THOMAS MERTON IN ALASKA

By Thomas Merton

THE ASIAN JOURNAL OF THOMAS MERTON

THE COLLECTED POEMS

EIGHTEEN POEMS

GANDHI ON NON-VIOLENCE

THE GEOGRAPHY OF LOGRAIRE

THE LITERARY ESSAYS

MY ARGUMENT WITH THE GESTAPO

NEW SEEDS OF CONTEMPLATION

RAIDS ON THE UNSPEAKABLE

SEEDS OF CONTEMPLATION

SELECTED POEMS

THE WAY OF CHUANG TZU

THE WISDOM OF THE DESERT

ZEN AND THE BIRDS OF APPETITE

About Thomas Merton

WORDS AND SILENCE: ON THE POETRY OF THOMAS MERTON
by Sister Thérèse Lentfoehr

Published by
New Directions

Thomas Merton
Thomas Merton in Alaska

Prelude to *The Asian Journal*
THE ALASKAN CONFERENCES, JOURNALS AND LETTERS

A New Directions Book

Acknowledgment is made to *Sisters Today* in which "This Is God's Work,"
"Prayer, Personalism, and the Spirit," "Building Community on God's Love,"
"Community, Politics, and Contemplation," "Prayer, Tradition, and Experience," "Prayer and Conscience," and "The Life that Unifies" first appeared
and to *The Priest* for "Prayer and the Priestly Tradition."

The journal and letters were edited by Robert E. Daggy for a limited, fine-
press edition designed and published as *The Alaskan Journal of Thomas Merton* by
Turkey Press in 1988. This material has now been combined with the conferences, or talks, Merton gave in Alaska, and first published as *Thomas Merton
in Alaska* clothbound and as New Directions Paperbook 652 in 1989.

New Directions thanks Turkey Press for their assistance in the preparation
of this edition and the use of their design and composition for the journals
and letters.

Published simultaneously in Canada by Penguin Books Canada Limited
Manufactured in the United States of America

Library of Congress Cataloging-in-Publication Data
Merton, Thomas, 1915–1968.
  Thomas Merton in Alaska.
  (New Directions paperbook; 652)
    1. Merton, Thomas, 1915–1968—Diaries. 2. Merton,
Thomas, 1915–1968—Correspondence. 3. Prayer.
4. Spiritual life—Catholic authors. I. Title.
BX4705.M542A3 1989   271'.125'024 [B]   87-24028
ISBN 0-8112-1048-0   ISBN 0-8112-1038-3 (pbk.)

New Directions Books are published for James Laughlin
by New Directions Publishing Corporation
80 Eighth Avenue, New York 10011

Contents

Preface

Books and articles about Thomas Merton continue to proliferate at a pace that keeps the bibliographers hopping, yet very little *original* Merton material remains unpublished. This is especially true of Merton's journal writing. During the last decade, starting with the posthumous publication of *The Asian Journal* in 1973, a number of separate and smaller editions of Merton's journals have appeared, gradually blocking in his final years—from roughly 1964, when Merton broke off *Conjectures of a Guilty Bystander*, to just a couple of days before his death in Bangkok. *The Alaskan Journal* carries on this tradition of illuminating Merton's self-reflections during an important time for him personally: a time of searching, growth, and change. Perhaps as significant, this two-week sequence covering Merton's travels in Alaska is, like *Day of a Stranger, Woods, Shore, Desert,* and *The Asian Journal* before it, the last of the journal writing that Merton clearly intended for general publication. All that now remains is a series of private notebooks and diaries (notably *Vow of Conversation*) whose futures rest in the hands of the Trustees of the Merton Legacy Trust.

The Alaskan Journal is somewhat unique among this cluster of Merton's late journal writing because of Robert Daggy's editorial decision to transcribe faithfully an actual working notebook.

Unlike *Woods, Shore, Desert*, Merton did not revise, rework, or polish his Alaskan notes for publication, nor has Dr. Daggy fleshed out Merton's syntax into a consistently fluid prose, a practice adopted (justifiably) by the editors of *The Asian Journal*. The entries in this edition of *The Alaskan Journal* appear as Merton jotted them down amid the inevitable distractions of travel, his language stripped down to the essence of his perceptions.

The Alaskan Journal is more than an item of Mertonia, more too than a comprehensive record of his Alaskan experience. It is a solid witness to Merton's extraordinary versatility. As a writer, Merton moves through these entries with a natural and unself-conscious freedom. He seems as comfortable with simply record-ing the events of the day as he is with fusing fragments from a newspaper into an anti-poem. Although spontaneous and some-what automatic in style, Merton still seeks, as if instinctively, for correspondences and symmetries amid seeming contradictions, as when "the excitements of the dead brain" (lifted from a quote out of *The Tibetan Book of the Dead*) fall into relief against the primordial cry of a baby on an airplane. The spontaneity of these notes makes for a liveliness and versatility, a freedom unencumbered by a conscious agenda. His reading in Alaska is versatile and eclectic too, from Orthodox Russian theology and Hermann Hesse to comic strips and graffiti in a toilet at the Anchorage airport. As a novice traveler and a man accustomed to the familiar routine of monastic life, Merton's rumblings around Alaska reflect a range of inter-personal skills which render him surprisingly at ease in all sorts of new situations, even when chatting with a barber about German hairdos. All of this is cut against the larger backdrop of Merton's temporal mobility, his search in space and time for a place of ideal solitude, and his spiritual quest, too, for personal peace during that bruising year, 1968.

It may well be that this versatility—captured so well here in these richly textured while starkly impressionistic notes—accounts for

Thomas Merton's popularity and appeal among such a broad spectrum of readers. That versatility might also explain Thomas Merton's inconsistencies and contradictions which continue to fuel interest and excite aggravation among those of us who have grown so close to him. Does the contemplative monk practice existential versatility or indulge in self-contradiction when waiting impatiently for his second Bloody Mary on an airplane? Merton spoke to a group of nuns in Alaska about the "complex self-contradictory temperament"—"of which I could tell you much," he said, "because that is a perfect description of me." What seemed to matter most during these final years was Merton's intensely private "struggle," as he noted in another journal, "to make the right adjustment in my own life," "the need for constant self-revision and growth, leaving behind the renunciations of yesterday and yet in continuity with all my yesterdays." He knew that struggle would be the subject of public misinterpretations and accusations of inconsistency. Nonetheless, in his own way and very much on his own terms, he persisted in his search for self-revision and personal growth. That might be why he went to Alaska and Asia, so excited by "a great sense of destiny, of being at last on my true way after years of waiting and wondering and fooling around."

David D. Cooper

Introduction
Ideal Solitude: The Alaskan Journal of Thomas Merton

In 1968, the last year of his life, Thomas Merton traveled more than he had since he entered the Cistercian Order in December, 1941. The trip to Asia in the Fall, with the posthumous publication of *The Asian Journal*, the continued emphasis on his interest in the East and Eastern religions, and his death in Bangkok, have tended to obscure—and probably rightly so—his earlier travels in 1968, even for those familiar with the Merton life.[1] Between May 16 and October 15, when he left for Asia, he visited California twice, New Mexico twice, Washington, D.C., Chicago, and Alaska. This final year of his life, a year of continuing searching and new experience, was a watershed period, different in tone and mood from what had gone before and most probably, had he not died, different from what would have come after. Merton himself indicates that he was seeking catharsis, searching for change. He wrote in his journal on September 9, two days before he left Gethsemani and Kentucky: "I go with a completely open mind. I hope without special illusions. My hope is simply to enjoy the long journey, profit by it, learn, change & perhaps find something or someone who will help me advance in my own spiritual quest. I am not starting out with a firm plan never to return or with an absolute determination to return at all costs. I do feel there is not much here for me at the moment & that I need to be open to lots of new possibilities. I hope I shall be! But I remain a monk of Gethsemani. Whether or not I will end my days here, I don't know—& perhaps it is not important. The great thing is to respond perfectly to God's will in this providential opportunity, whatever it may bring."[2]

These pre-Asia trips, particularly those to the American West and to that newest of frontiers, Alaska, were potentially significant to the Merton "journey," to the Merton "quest," even if not so immediately and apparently so as the Asian trip. Asia may have been uppermost in Merton's thoughts[3]—he may have been, as he noted on August 22, having pipedreams about Bhutan and tea plantations near Darjeeling—it may have been (and undoubtedly was) in Asia that *he* thought catharsis would take place—but other considerations, some quite practical ones in view of Merton's stage in his life and thinking, were important too.

These other trips, after the fatal development in Bangkok, have not seemed perhaps significant, have not received the coverage they would have if Merton had returned and become a "monk of Gethsemani" in California, New Mexico, or Alaska. This occurred in part because there was more information on the Asian trip and because that information was more readily available. Though Merton prepared the journal of his spring jaunts to California and New Mexico for publication, calling it *Woods, Shore, Desert: A Notebook, May 1968* and leaving it with James Laughlin, publisher of New Directions, before he left for Asia, it was not published until 1983—ten years after *The Asian Journal* was transcribed and edited from his journals and published.[4] The other portions of his journals, after it was decided not to include them in *The Asian Journal*, have remained unpublished until the appearance of the Alaskan portions in this edition.

These other considerations centered on what Merton might do with his life *after* he returned from Asia. He gave conferences, workshops and retreats, he spoke and lectured on these trips, but a large part of the purpose for them, in the United States as well as possibly in Asia, was for Merton to explore, to observe, to "scout out" places where he (and perhaps other monks) might enjoy more solitude, more seclusion, more isolation than had developed for him at Gethsemani, even in the Hermitage. Brother Patrick Hart pointed out in his Foreword to *Woods, Shore, Desert*: "After the abbatial election [in 1968], Merton began discussing with the new Abbot [Father Flavian Burns] the possibilities of a more isolated hermitage in view of the fact that the present one was too accessible to retreatants, old friends, and casual visitors. Under the new legislation, it was now possible to live in a hermitage at some distance from one's monastery, even in a foreign country, as two monks of Gethsemani have subsequently done, one in Mexico and another in Papua New Guinea."[5]

Except for hospital stays, visits to the doctor, and two brief trips, Merton had literally not left Gethsemani in nearly twenty-seven years.[6] Travel had been considered inimical to the monastic life. His Abbot from 1948 to 1968, Dom James Fox, had generally discouraged travel. Merton noted on June 12, 1964, when he learned that he might meet with the celebrated Zen scholar, D. T. Suzuki, in New York: "After writing as I did the other day that I thought even temporary travel would be useless to think about . . . I thought it was important enough to ask the Abbot's permission. I certainly did not think that Dom James would give this permission and yet, very hesitantly, he did."[7] Merton himself had eschewed travel, consistently and firmly refusing invitations to speak, hold workshops, and make appearances, usually without consulting the Abbot while frequently excusing himself by saying that the Abbot refused to let him go.

Change had taken place in the Order and the former strictures against travel had relaxed. In some informal remarks at Santa Barbara, just after leaving Alaska, he said: "I am out of the monastery for the first time in about twenty-five years, with the permission of a new Abbot, who sort of fell out of the clouds into this position of authority in a very providential kind of way. The old Abbot . . . was very strong on my not leaving the monastery and going anywhere, or anybody leaving the monastery and going anywhere, and he became a hermit, which is what I've been for the last ten years, and his first act was to attend Robert Kennedy's funeral, which got us all off the hooks that we were on about traveling."[8] It was true that the new Abbot, Flavian Burns, was more receptive to Merton's traveling, but it is also true that Merton himself was at a point where he was ready, even anxious, to travel.

Despite rumors, then and now, he had no intention of leaving the Order or of severing connection with Gethsemani. He tried to squelch such rumors in his "Circular Letter" to his friends, written shortly before he left Gethsemani in September.[9] He noted in his journal that he remained a "monk of Gethsemani." He wrote to Brother Patrick Hart from Alaska on September 26: "Keep telling everyone that I am a monk of Gethsemani and intend to remain one all my days." Yet, as Brother Patrick has pointed out, this phrase, under the new legislation, suddenly took on a new and different meaning. The possibility now loomed that Merton might be a monk of Gethsemani and yet live as a hermit at some distance from Gethsemani, even possibly outside the United States. A "monk of Gethsemani" might now be nowhere near the actual location Gethsemani. Taken in this light, Merton's assertions with their ring of commitment did not actually commit him to any one course for he might have become a "monk of Gethsemani" in New Mexico, Alaska, or on that tea plantation near Darjeeling.

Merton took off on his travels with enthusiasm and boyish optimism. It is clear that he went to Alaska with that "open mind" of which he had spoken. He had already toyed with the idea of being a "monk of Gethsemani" in Alaska. On August 22, he recorded in his journal: "A picture of Mount McKinley . . . I cannot believe that

I may see it. Or even find myself one day living near it." He continued by asking: "Is Alaska a real option? One would think not." Yet he seems to have kept himself open to the Alaskan possibility, becoming so enthralled with Alaska (while he was in Alaska) that he wavered close to commitment. He described Alaska in glowing terms in his journal and his letters—"terrific," "fabulous," "grand." He concluded after flying around Alaska that it might be a spot where one could find an atmosphere conducive to solitude. He wrote to Abbot Burns: "There is no question that this place is full of ideal solitude in every form." Later he wrote to him: "This would be the obvious place to settle for real solitude in the United States."

Merton, however, despite his enthusiasm—he seems always to have been enthusiastic about a place while he was there or about a project while he was working on it—was somewhat ambivalent, somewhat wary of commitment. One senses this in his journal and in his letters. The thought of bears, with which Alaska abounds, made him nervous. And one gets the feeling that Alaska, or at least some parts of it, was too isolated, too wild, too remote for hermit Merton. His ambivalence stemmed in part undoubtedly from his reluctance to make any decision about what would happen after Asia before he went to Asia. He does conclude that it would have been "folly" for him *not* to consider Alaska, but he wrote to Burns that he wished to wait until after his return before deciding. He even thought another trip to Alaska might be necessary.

It is also true that, though Merton claimed a grasp of the situation, his enthusiasm and tendency to think he was able to assess a situation quickly and in depth after only a cursory exposure caused him frequently to react, almost to overreact, too positively. As Monica Furlong points out: "Dom Flavian feels that Merton was not always very practical in assessing the pros and cons."[10] Alexander Lipski feels that Merton's idealism and enthusiasm led him to a naive, all-accepting, and uncritical evaluation of many things on the Asian trip.[11] This probably happened in Alaska as well.

Merton also was impatient to be on his way to Asia. He noted on September 23, with over a week left to stay in Alaska: "I thumb through my tickets to Los Angeles, Honolulu, Bangkok, Calcutta, Katmandu . . . and am eager to get going." In many ways, these preliminary trips with the workshops and the talks were a distraction, an impediment to the Asian pilgrimage. He said in Santa Barbara after leaving Alaska: "I have a feeling that I am about to go to Asia without having caught up on the amount of meditation I ought to do. I've just been running around Alaska wildly."[12]

It is clear that Merton liked Alaska, that he thought about the possibilities of living there, or at least he thought about it *while* he was there. This part of his trip doubtless helped to prepare him, a man unused to travel for more than twenty years, for the more arduous and longer Asian stint. We shall, of course, never know, since he died in Bangkok, whether Merton would ever have become a "monk of Gethsemani" in Alaska. He did say: "If I am to be a hermit in the U.S., Alaska is probably the place for it." Parts of Alaska definitely appealed to him. When Lake Aleknagik "spoke" to him and he answered, "Is this it?" he did not know that it would not be it, that a different destiny lay ahead. But his brief experience in Alaska was a positive and enjoyable one. After it, the monk of Gethsemani was off to California and Asia convinced that Alaska would provide "ideal solitude" in the United States.

I first assembled Thomas Merton's Alaskan journal and letters for a fine limited edition entitled *The Alaskan Journal* brought out in 1988 by Harry and Sandra Reese of Turkey Press in Isla Vista, California. The present New Directions' book includes this material as well as the conferences (talks) Merton gave in Alaska.

The Alaskan Journal was transcribed and compiled from the two notebooks (the "personal" journal, #40, and the public journal, #36) on file in the Thomas Merton Studies Center of Bellarmine

College. Material from the public and personal journals has been dovetailed together in much the same way that the editors compiled *The Asian Journal*. It was hard to see the distinction between the two except that the public journal is slightly fuller, more detailed, and perhaps a bit rougher. The entries in the personal journal precede entries made in Asia which were included in *The Asian Journal*. Sixteen letters, on file in the Center, have been added to supplement Merton's journal entries.

Robert E. Daggy

Part One

The Alaskan Journal and Letters

Prologue / *Gethsemani*

June 7

> *Time in Alaska*
>> Juneau–Pacific Standard
>> Yukon Standard
>> Alaska Standard–Anchorage & Fairbanks
>> Bering Sea Time–Nome

※

August 22

A PICTURE of Mount McKinley in front of me under the lamp—
(came today as a feast day greeting for Sunday)—I cannot believe
that I may see it. Or even find myself one day living near it. Is
Alaska a real option? One would think not. And yet there's that
Bishop . . . Certainly it is not the place I myself would spontane-
ously choose (full of military!).

For myself—Bhutan! Or that tea-plantation I heard about yesterday near Darjeeling!

※

August 26

THE EMBASSY CLUB which (though the food was O.K.) struck me as
the epitome of all that is stupid & expensive about suburbia.[1] All
the organ playing, the dull wives, the smell of money, the aura

I

of boredom & phoniness, the expensive unattractive clothes. The general plush ugliness of everything. Giving me some inkling of how utterly horrible things must now be back "home" in Douglaston or Great Neck! (or, my God, Alaska!)

⁂

August 27

LETTER from the Archbishop of Anchorage.[2] The Vicar General[3] will meet me at the plane—Northwestern Flight 3 from Chicago is the best—several pieces of property in mind. I can live in a trailer at the (contemplative) Precious Blood Nuns . . .

Itinerary

Tuesday, *September 17*	Chicago to Anchorage
Wednesday, *September 18*	Eagle River [Convent of the Precious Blood]
Thursday, *September 19*	Eagle River
Friday, *September 20*	Eagle River
Saturday, *September 21*	Eagle River—Ft. Richardson Elemendorf Air Force Base
Sunday, *September 22*	Eagle River
Monday, *September 23*	Cordova
Tuesday, *September 24*	Valdez—Copper Valley Matanuska Valley—Anchorage
Wednesday, *September 25*	Anchorage
Thursday, *September 26*	Anchorage—Palmer
Friday, *September 27*	Anchorage—Yakutat—Juneau
Saturday, *September 28*	Juneau—Anchorage
Sunday, *September 29*	Anchorage
Monday, *September 30*	Anchorage—Dillingham
Tuesday, *October 1*	Dillingham—Anchorage
Wednesday, *October 2*	Anchorage to San Francisco
Thursday, *October 3*	San Francisco to Santa Barbara

Fine snowcovered mountains lift their knowledges out a gap of clouds, + I am exhilarated with them. Salute the spirit dwelling. Spirit-lifting came up out of the invisible land. The little boy next is playing his telephone.

+

First sight of mountains of Alaska, strongly ribbed, through cloud.
Superb blue of the gulf - indescribable in pattern. Bird wings, vast, mottled, long black streamers, curves, seismatoz, lyre bird tails.

+

I am here in answer to someone's prayer.

+

Sept. 18. Eagle River - Alaska - the convent of the Precious Blood - surrounded by woods, with a highway (too) near.
The woods of Alaska - marvelous - deep in wet peat, ferns, rotten fallen trees big-leaved thorn scrub, yellowing birch, stunted fir, aspens. Thick, ~~this~~ thronid bush. Smelling of lefs + of rot. Rich undergrowth full of mosses, berries - + probably (in other seasons) flowers. The air is now here cool and sharp as late November in the 'outside' (i.e. 'the States') ('lower 48)

+

The convent chapel looks out through big windows at beech, a purple + green mountainside. Quiet. Sense of belonging here. The spirit of the community is good. They will move to a better site. This is a nice house but has 'a water problem.'

+

I turn a page. The eagle feather dropped by one of the Apache murrues, slides, rotates, across the ~~little~~ ~~wit~~ flight desk.

+

Priests of Alaska, friendly, generous. After the workshop will look for place.

A single page from Merton's Alaskan notebook dated September 18, 1968

The Alaskan Journal

September 17

CHICAGO was rainy. Celebrated the F. of the Stigmatization of St. Francis at the new Poor Clare convent—After talking to them the evening before. Wind. View of woods on one side. Distant city on the other.

First—went down to see the old empty convent on S. Loftus Street. High brick walls, empty corridors, brick courtyard. Church with no more adoration.

＊

We took off an hour late, big plane full of children, heading for Anchorage, Tokyo & Seoul. Flew up slowly out of the dark into the brilliant light, this Bardo of pure sky. (Clouds full of planes seeking Chicago in the dark.)

＊

Bardo Thödöl—your own true nature confronts you as Pure Truth, "subtle, sparkling, bright, dazzling, glorious, and radiantly awesome like a mirage moving across a landscape in springtime . . . Be not terrified . . . From the midst of that radiance the natural sound of Reality, reverberating like a thousand thunders simultaneously sounding, will come. That is the natural sound of thine own real self. Be not daunted thereby nor terrified. . . ."[4]

Hot towels. Man (Peace Corps) talking about Bangkok, Singapore, learning awareness, State Dept., to one of the mothers—his wife Japanese? A beautiful little baby which she keeps lifting up over her head (but now feeding from bottle).

❊

"Hermit cells" in PC monastery. The Red Barn nearby. The man in the grey shirt crouching in the wood (Cleveland—a bar owner, bartender, whore & another, kidnapped, shot in the park, found by joggers). The old PC convent. Sister with an ulcered leg feared that if the convent were left unguarded teen-agers would break in the graveyard & dig up the dead.

❊

Bardo Thödöl   "The experiencing of reality"
After missing the clear light: 4 days, 4 Buddhas, 4 nights.

    water—white light of Akshobhya
                anger—makes one fly to "dull
                smoke colored light of hell"

    earth—yellow light of Ratna-Sambhava
                egotism—"preference for dull
                blueish light from human world"

    fire—red light of Amitabha
                attachment—dull red light of
                Preta-loka

    air—green light of Amogha-Siddhi
                jealousy—dull green—Asura-loka
                (quarreling & warfare)

But—"The forty-two perfectly endowed deities issuing from within thy heart, being the product of thine own pure love, will come to shine. Know them!"[5]

"If thou art frightened by the pure radiance of Wisdom & attracted by the impure lights of the six Lokas . . . thou wilt be whirled round and round (in Sangsara[6]) & made to taste the suffering thereof."[7]

❧

Meanwhile however there was something impressive about the old empty rooms & corridors, with here & there an ancient statue lamenting the emptiness, the dark. One felt that it was a place where prayer had "been valid." Even the old brick walls of the outside were impressive.

And this morning old Sr. Margaret was starting out in the rain to go begging (for food, in stores).

❧

A while ago we were over miles of Canadian lakes, blue, blue-green, & brown, with woods between, an occasional road. Still three hours from Anchorage. Two—probably from Alaska. Clouds again, packed thick, quilted, beneath us.

❧

I borrowed the letters of Miller & Durrell[8] from Ron S.[9] & don't feel like reading them. The first one, with Durrell putting down *Ulysses*[10] (saying *Tropic of Cancer* was better) turned me off.

(More lakes down below, between clouds. Olive green, wild stretches of watery land.)

⁂

The young Apaches were racing to give back energy to the sun. The clan that was fastest was the best painted & their first [runner] was like an African antelope with long yellow streamers flying from his head & a mirror in the center of his forehead.

⁂

From Knowledge-Holders each "holding a crescent knife & skull filled with blood, dancing & making the *mudra* of fascination."[11]
  Glad to be not in Kentucky. But here over this blanket of cold cloud hiding lakes.
  The bands of the Mothers, the Dakinis,[12] sliding upon solid cloud.

Ecce dabit voci suam vocem virtutis date glorinum Deo super Israel: magnificentia eius et virtus eius in nubibus.
                                                            —*Psalm 67*

(The wrathful deities[13] are peaceful deities returning in menacing form, blood drinkers, emerging from the excitements of the dead brain) ("recognition — of one's own self in such forms! — becometh more difficult!")
  The high plane[14] over the north is a dinning *orchestra* of conch shells, thigh bone trumpets, drums, cymbals—a lama orchestra such as one hears when pressing shut the ears. Also a cosmic hissing—not to mention the crying of babies and the gabble of human conversation (and afternoon perfumes).
  Shades close out the Canada sun, the afternoon & the brute big

shining masses of the jet engines stand out fiercely blue-black above the cloud.

"At the same time a dull blue light from the brute world will come to shine along with the Radiance of Wisdom . . ."[15]

❧

Flight yoga. Training in cosmic colors.

Dull, concise bronze of ginger ale.

Last night, choosing the scotch Fr. Xavier[16] offered was as silly as a choice of smoke, & I had smoke in my head when I awoke.

Ginger ale has in it perfume of stewardess.

In the war-plane's music, the natural sound of truth thunders —but very differently. Equivocally.

❧

Cries of "Slay, slay & awe-inspiring mantras . . . [but] flee not."[17] I close my eyes & see the colors of Indian blankets.

❧

The little Japanese baby cries with a fine clear shining cry, pro-longed, unchoking, a curving repeated descant, well punctuated with good breaths.

❧

The black falsely jeweled souvenir aprons of the Indian runners.

Fine snow covered mountains lift their knowledges into a gap of clouds & I am exhilarated with them. Salute the spirit dwellings. Spirit-liftings come up out of the invisible land. The little boy also is playing his telephone.

❦

First sight of mountains of Alaska, strongly ribbed, through cloud. Superb blue of the gulf, indescribable ice patterns. Bird wings, vast, mottled, long black streamers, curves, scimitars, lyre bird tails.

❦

I am here in answer to someone's prayer.

❦

September 18 / Eagle River

ALASKA—the Convent of the Precious Blood—surrounded by woods, with a highway (too) near. The woods of Alaska—marvelous—deep in wet grass, fern, rotten fallen trees, big-leaved thorn scrub, yellowing birch, stunted fir, aspens. Thick. Humid. Lush. Smelling of life & of rot. Rich undergrowth, full of mosses, berries —& probably (in other seasons) flowers. The air is now here cool and sharp as late November in the "outside" (i.e. "the States") ("lower 48").

❦

The convent chapel looks out through big windows at birch, a purple & green mountainside. Quiet.

Sense of belonging here. The spirit of the community is good.
They will move to a better site. This is a nice house but has "a
water problem."

✤

I turn a page. The eagle feather dropped by one of the Apache
runners, slides, volatile, across the slick desk.

✤

Priests of Alaska, friendly, generous. After the workshop will look
for places.

> Cordova & Fr. Llorente.[18]
>
> Valdez.
>
> Islands.
>
> A place looking at "The Big One" (McKinley)
>
> A place called what—Hutchinson? Cunningham?
>> No. Dillingham. Now in the
>> same time zone as Anchorage.

✤

MOSAIC: ALASKA PAPER & FUNNIES

Burning bon fires review by Assembly
A borough ordinance will face junkheap or major overhaul
Split assembly into snarling rural & urban
Camps writes Stephen Brent of our News
Staff. And in Dallas
Wallace[19] had a big day Tuesday
Dramatic increase "He's moving up
Fast" said a strategist and

"Garbage burned further away
Would be prohibited if
It created a nuisance"—
"When I was Governor of Alabama I met
Nelson Rockefeller & George Romney & some
Of those others & they didn't impress me."
Then four died in
Alaska planes
(Skwentna River
Kenai Penin.
Sula)
"He passed over the smoke in an attempt
To see where it was coming from."
And it was from Curtis LeMay[20]
Speaking in the Anchorage Westward Hotel.

Also in Kenai
Many are now
Wearing Wallace buttons.

Gavora 37 owns the Market Basket Supermarket in Fairbanks.
And ferry service between Alaska & Seattle
Will be doubled.
A post is filled.
A Time Zone is changed.
Next Sunday
A Fall Dance is held
With music furnished by
Fantastic Zoot & Bros.
Gundy Rose.
The public is invited
To hear Sen. Nick Begich[21]
(And of course Gen. Curtis LeMay
On Vietnam)
(Funnies)

"Come I will take you to my Uncle who was fired."
"Good."
"Uncle Salvador
Senor Sawyer is not
What we thought."
"Something is wrong at the mine."
Uncle Salvador remains proud
And turns away (Thinks:) "You'll get
No help from me!"
Says: "Why are they flooding
The exploratory channel
At the 3700 foot level?"

Tigers win pennant
Drenched in champagne while
Crowds in darkness chant
"We want Tigers."
On this day (Wednesday Sept 18)
Aries shall "utilize showmanship
Dress up product" & Taurus should
"Strive to be specific—no beating
Around the bush." Gemini "be complete
Not fragmentary." LIBRA
(Well frankly it's a good day for Libra with "a Virgo individual
Tonight")
"Romantic interests are spurred..."
All is glamor today for lucky
Libra. And Scorpio should stop grumbling
"About overtime."
And final word
To Aries "Compile facts."
As to Aquarius (my own
Self in workshop) "Necessity of public
Relations. Some around you are ultra-
Sensitive. Older person

Wants to be heard!" (I pray that's Mother Rita Mary!)
Russian space ship returns from moon.
Helicopter shot down in Vietnam.
Students rioting in Mexico City (for days).
Fair today, high in fifties (again).
Turned it off before the football news came on.

✤

First Ecstasy of Rama Krishna [22]

One day in June or July when he was six years old he was walking along a narrow path between ricefields, eating puffed rice from a basket. He looked up at the sky & saw a beautiful storm cloud, & a flight of snow white cranes passing in front of it, above him. He lost consciousness & fell into a faint at the beauty of it. A peasant found him with rice scattered all about & carried him home.

✤

September 19 / Alaska
Louisville—Christ of the Desert—Jicarilla Apache Reservation—Santa Fe—Chicago—Anchorage—Eagle River Convent.

I am now here on a bright cold morning & the first thin dust of snow is on the lower hills. Mt. McKinley is visible in the distance from the Precious Blood Convent. Next to which I live in a trailer (very comfortable).

✤

On the morning of the 10th I went down to the monastery for the last time to get some money, pick up mail, say goodbye to Fr. Flavian, Bros. Maurice, Patrick. [23] No one else much knew anything

14

about my departure. Ron Seitz came about ten. A grey, cool, fall morning. We drove into Louisville. I got travellers checks, medicine in St. Matthews. An AWOL bag for camera, second pair of shoes, etc. Afternoon—a shower & short rest at O'Callaghan's[24] in the evening a supper send-off party that probably could have been better done without. But no matter. Dan Walsh[25] was there & I hadn't seen him for a long time. I slept at St. Bonaventure's Friary[26] & got out early in the morning. Flew to Chicago then Albuquerque.

I was met at the airport in Albuquerque by Tom Carlyle[27] a very likeable hippie type who is staying at Christ of the Desert & working for them. A really good, sincere, spiritual person. One of the best. We drove up in his Volkswagen—dragging a plaster mixer with which he plans to make adobe brick for the monks.

Two days retreat in the canyon. Swam in the cold Chama.

Then to the Jicarilla Apache encampment feast on the reservation near Dulce. A feast of Tabernacles. Booths of boughs, tents & campfires everywhere. Then the race the next day. Back to Santa Fe. Slept at the Devereux's in Reyena Madre. Low adobe house. Supper at the Pink Adobe—good curry but too much of it.

Flew from Albuquerque to Chicago (last sight of distant Pedernal quite clear!) Rain in Chicago. Went to the new Poor Clare convent & gave them a talk; I liked the architecture. Ed Noonan the architect came for mass next day—I concelebrated with Fr. Xavier Carroll, who took me to the plane, with one of the sisters who was leaving.

The Northwest plane for Anchorage, Tokyo & Seoul was late getting started. Crowded with families, American & Japanese, returning to Asia. I felt for the first time that Asia was getting close!

My flight to Alaska was mostly over clouds. Quiet. A soldier on

15

the outside seat; the middle seat of the three empty, we didn't talk much except for a little bit just before landing. (He said Anchorage wasn't any colder in winter than Syracuse, NY, but that there was a lot of snow.)

The clouds opened over Mt. St. Elias & after that I was overwhelmed by the vastness, the patterns of glaciers, the burnished copper sheen of the sun on the bright blue sea. The shore line. The bare purple hills. The high mountains full of snow, the dark islands stark in the sun—burnish on the water.

We swung slowly down into Anchorage & got out into cold, clear autumn air. Everywhere the leaves have turned. Gold of the aspens & birches everywhere.

Without actually going into Anchorage we (Fr. [John] Lunney met me) drove out on Route 1 to the convent, at Eagle River.

It is a nice house among the birches, at the foot of low mountains, looking out through the trees toward Cook Inlet & Mount McKinley—the nuns may move in a few months as the place is not quite suitable.

I have a sense of great warmth & generosity in the clergy here. The Archbishop is away at Juneau, but will be back next week— all are very eager to help & I feel they are eager to have me settle here. Meanwhile I'm busy on a workshop with the nuns. They are a good community, & like all, they have their troubles.

⁂

This afternoon—in the sun at the foot of a birch, in the bushes near the monastery, at a point where you can see Mt. McKinley & Mt. Foraker—great, silent & beautiful presence in the afternoon sun.

⁂

September 21 / Eagle River

"ONE WILL UNDERSTAND the extent to which the anthropological realities of our everyday experiences are deformed by sin and correspond little to the pure norms of the new creation which is being realized in the Church. Actually, the individual who possesses a part of nature and reserves it for himself, the subject who defines himself by opposition to all that which is not 'I,' is not the person or hypostasis who shares nature in common with others and who exists as person in a positive relationship to other persons. Self-will . . . is not identical to the will of the new creation—to the will which one finds in renouncing oneself, in the unity of the Body of Christ, wherein the canons of the Church make us recognize a common and individual will. Not the properties of an individual nature, but the unique relationship of each being with God—a relationship by the Holy Spirit and realized in grace—is what constitutes the uniqueness of a human person."[28]

☙

September 22

SUNDAY. 6 a.m. on KHAR Anchorage; Alaskan Golden Nugget Potatoes respectfully suggest that we worship God since we are a nation under God & want to build a stronger America. Nugget Potatoes are glad of this opportunity to "voice this thinking." A good thought from a respectful potato.

☙

Yesterday—end of workshop—visit of P. Blood priests—not without a song & Ole Man River. Evening—to the army base at Ft. Richardson—like city of shiny apartments—bourbon on the rocks

—tarpon fishing on TV—wild ducks in slow motion flight—
memories of Brooklyn. And supper at the AF base at Elmendorf
(like city of shiny apartments). Heated argument between conservative & progressive clergy & laity: Which is better: to kneel
for communion or to stand?

⚜

September 23

ANCHORAGE DAILY NEWS advises Aquarius to read travel folders.
I thumb through my tickets to Los Angeles, Honolulu, Bangkok,
Calcutta, Katmandu . . . and am eager to get going.

Climbed a mountain behind the convent, & looked out over the
vast valley—Mt. McKinley—the Alaska Range—far off Redoubt
Volcano & Iliamna.

Today I go to Cordova.

⚜

Graffiti in toilet—Anchorage Airport.

On the whole much more tame than usual.

For instance: "Vote for Nixon—(spelled NIXION)"
"Peace & good will to your fellow men!"

Someone declares he is on his way to Vietnam.

Another states:
"Missouri is best."

Which draws the only dirty comment:
"For assholes."

On the whole a very genteel set of announcements & no
pictorial matter.

Another graffiti "Hickel has crabs" (Hickel[29] is the governor).

⚜

September 23 / Cordova

LANDED at the cool, lovely airfield shortly after dawn. Still freezing. I rode into town on the airport bus—a school bus—with a bunch of duck hunters, very voluble about their luck & about the good weather which is bad for them as the ducks & geese have not begun to move south.

Ducks in the water of the Copper River Delta.

⚜

I find St. Joseph's Church, no one around. I walk in the rectory & after a while Fr. Llorente arrives—a remarkable person, a Spanish Jesuit who got himself sent to the Yukon 30 years ago & has been in Alaska ever since—has become a sort of legend in the region. He was going to leave to work with Mexican migrants in California, but was needed for Cordova . . . He stayed.

A small fishing town between steep mountains & blue water— a highway on one side, & Eyak Lake around at the back.

I have no hesitation in saying Eyak Lake seemed perfect in many ways—for a place to live. The quiet end of it is several miles back in the mountains, completely isolated, silent. Wild geese were feeding there. Great silver salmon were turning red & dying in shallows where they had spawned (some had been half eaten by bears). Bears would be the only problem but Fr. Llorente said they were not grizzlies. A few cabins nearer town were attractive. Also the bay was impressive.

Other ideas of Fr. Llorente: Yakutat & a shrine (abandoned) of the Little Flower outside Juneau (many sea lions there).

❧

Plans had been for me to go to Kenai Peninsula & Kodiak tomorrow but I am going to Matanuska Valley instead.

❧

September 24 / Valdez (Valdeez)

AT THE FAR END of a long blue arm of water, full of islands. The bush pilot flies low over the post office thinking it to be the Catholic Church—to alert the priest we are arriving.

The old town of Valdez, wrecked by earthquake, tidal wave. Still some buildings leaning into shallow salt water. Others, with windows smashed by a local drunkard. I think I have lost the roll of film I took in Valdez & the mountains (from the plane).

❧

Most impressive mountains I have seen in Alaska: Drum & Wrangell & the third great massive one whose name I forget, rising out of the vast birchy plain of Copper Valley. They are sacred & majestic mountains, ominous, enormous, noble, stirring. You want to attend to them. I could not keep my eyes off them. Beauty & terror of the Chugach. Dangerous valleys. Points. Saws. Snowy nails.

❧

NOISES as the bishop's house awakes—noise of heat tapping in the walls, of water running, of plates being set, of the feet of domestic prelates on carpeted floors, creaking of floorboards where there is movement overhead to left & to right. Feet on stairs. Cutlery. Crockery. Planes coming down to FAA airport beyond the birches outside.

❦

Today I fly to Juneau with Archbishop Ryan. Then to Ketchikan tomorrow & back to Anchorage Saturday.

Sound of chapel door closing as Bishop comes down to say his office before breakfast (Mass tonight—concelebration in Juneau).

The bishop's house is warm & quiet. It smells of bacon.

❦

Plane grounded. We cannot go to Juneau where the Archbishop had planned a clergy conference & concelebration this evening. Flight tomorrow perhaps to Yakutat.

❦

Haircut in Anchorage Westward Hotel. Manuel, an artist in hairstyles, found little to do on me, but spoke of what he had learned about wigs in Heidelberg. "Inexpensive!" He emphasized this. A nasty hint!

❦

The Bishop is tired & will go to rest — which is only right. I write postcards & letters. Letter to Fr. Flavian on an electric type-writer in the Chancery Office (second one. A better report than yesterday's).

✦

I walk briefly through the streets of Anchorage, viewing the huge lift of land after the 1964 earthquake, looking out at the barges drilling for oil in Cook Inlet. The mountains to the west are hidden in fog & snow clouds. Behind the city, the tops are powdered with clean snow.

✦

I have a reservation for San Francisco on the 2nd. Plan to sleep there. A letter came from Suzanne B.[30] so maybe I'll have supper with her. She said she had read in Ralph Gleason's column that I had left the monastery & was going to Tibet. October 3rd I am supposed to go on to Santa Barbara, & have a conference at the Center on the 4th (No—3rd).

✦

Behind Palmer: Pioneer Peak, badly named, tall & black & white in the snow — mist, rugged armatures, indestructible, great. It vanishes into snow cloud as we retreat up the valley into birch flats. McKinley hidden.

The log house of Mr. & Mrs. Peck by the windy lake. Clouds of blowing aspen & birch leaves fly across the lawn. Mr. Peck with an army field jacket & a good Dutch cigar — brought by the big silent boy from KLM who sits with a bottle of bourbon in the shadows of the kitchen.

*

Mrs. Peck's sister has half finished an enormous jigsaw puzzle which occupies a whole table. Mrs. Peck, a lovely, ageless Eskimo woman, plump, broad Asian smile, like the faces of Nepalese tribes in the book I saw today (Anchorage Public Library).

*

September 27 / Yakutat

BAY with small islands. Driving rain on the docks. A few fishing boats. Beat-up motorboats, very poor. An old battered green rowboat called *The Jolly Green Giant.*

It is a village of Indians, with an FAA station nearby. Battered houses. A small Indian girl opens the door of the general store. Looks back at us as we pass. Cannery buildings falling down. Old tracks are buried in mud & grass. A dilapidated building was once a "roundhouse" though it is a large rectangle. After that, all there is is a long straight gravel road pointing in the mist between tall hemlocks out into the nowhere where more of the same will be extended to a lumber operation. The woods are full of moose, & black bear, & brown bear, & even a special bear found only at Yakutat — the glacier bear (or blue bear).

Frank Ryman had in his lodge the skin of a wolf — as big as a small bear.

Yakutat has plenty of wolves & coyotes, besides bears.

And in the village are many murders.

Tlingit Indians.

Here there was once a Russian penal colony. It was wiped out by the Indians.

Yakutat—one of the only—perhaps *the* only place that is on Yukon time. All the other places have adopted one of the other timebelts, Anchorage or Pacific.

⚜

September 27 / Juneau

ALONE in the empty bishop's house at Juneau (he[31] has retired—the see is vacant) after concelebration, dinner, & conference at the Cathedral. Driving rain, & a long spectacular thin waterfall down the side of the mountain becomes, in a concrete channel outside the house, the fastest torrent I have ever seen. It must be running fifty miles an hour into the choppy bay.

⚜

This morning—we flew in bad weather to Yakutat, came down out of thick clouds on to a shore full of surf & hemlock & muskeg. Desolate airstrip.

Frank Ryman drove us into the village to show me the village. Broken down houses, mostly inhabited by Tlingit Indians, an old fish cannery, & a small dock with a few fishing boats on a lovely broad bay with islands. Everything seemed covered with hemlock. Driving rain, mountains invisible. Frank Ryman has a quarter acre of land he offered me — & it is enough to put a trailer on. But

24

it is right at the edge of the village. If I lived there I would become very involved in the life of the village and would probably become a sort of pastor.

⚡

We left Yakutat after dinner (at Ryman's "lodge" out at the airstrip), flew in rain to Juneau which turns out to be a fascinating place clinging to the feet of several mountains at the edge of a sort of fjord. I never saw such torrential rain as met us when we got out of the plane!

⚡

Earlier in the week; visit Cordova on Monday. The road that goes around to the back of Eyak Lake is one of the most beautiful places in Alaska—silent, peaceful, among high mountains, wild geese & ducks on the flats. Perhaps in many ways the best place I have seen so far. The bay there, too, is magnificent.

⚡

Tuesday we flew with a bush pilot—over the mountains & glaciers to Valdez. Then up through the pass in the Chugach to Copper Valley & Copper Center school, with the Wrangell Mountains beyond it. And down again through the Matanuska Valley to Anchorage.

⚡

Generous hospitality of Archbishop Ryan in Anchorage. I have been staying at his house since Tuesday night. A comfortable bed in the basement where he also has his bar. He is from New York & has a New York humor & urbanity.

✦

Whatever else I may say—it is clear I like Alaska much better than Kentucky & it seems to me that if I am to be a hermit in the U.S., Alaska is probably the place for it. The SE is good—rain & all. I have still to go out to Western Alaska—& missed Kodiak where there is, I hear, an old Russian hermit. (Last week I saw the Russian church in the Indian village of Eklutna, up the road from the convent.)

✦

Last Sunday I climbed a mountain behind the convent, guided by a boy who knew the trail. Very tired after it!

✦

Wednesday & Thursday—wrote letters in the Chancery Office at Anchorage, two of them to Fr. Flavian, trying to describe Alaska.

✦

September 28 / Juneau

GREEN WALLS of mountains in the rain. Lights of the Federal Building in rainy dusk. Narrow streets ending up against a mountain. A towering waterfall snaking down out of the clouds. Green.

Bluegreen Juneau. The old cathedral. The deserted hospital. The deserted hotel. The deserted dock. The deserted school. We met Senator Gruening[32] in the airport & shook his hand. Famous people are never as tall as you expect.

❧

Night in the comfortable bishop's house. Torrent in the channel outside. Sound of water racing smooth & even at fifty miles an hour into the bay. I oversleep. Get up just in time to put a few clothes on — but not to shower — before Fr. Manske[33] arrives (7:30) with the car to take me out along the shore. The clouds lift a little & beyond the green islands are vague, snowcovered peaks. A beautiful channel full of islands.

❧

September 29 / St. Michael

QUIET SUNDAY morning in the (empty) bishop's house. Anchorage. Rain. Wet carpet of fallen birch leaves. Wind. Gulls. Long road going off past a gravelpit toward Providence Hospital where I preached a day of recollection today. More & more leaves fall. Everyone's at Palmer, celebrating St. Michael & the Parish.

❧

Talking of the changing of nun's names (at Mother House) Sister Charity said: *"Those who have mysteries have to change."* Others were interested in the rigors of Trappist life, sleeping in underwear. A Kodiak grey nun knew Abbot Obrecht. There's always someone, somewhere who knows a Trappist.

Noise of heat walking around in the walls. I am hungry.

❧

The empty house of bishops. Quiet. False flowers & false autumn weeds in a bunch on the table. Empty coke can. Two Sundays ago I was driving down from the Jicarilla reservation to Santa Fe. One Sunday ago tired from climbing the mountain at Eagle River.

❧

"All the Sisters who have mysteries have to be changed?" And they are delighted at my monastic nickname "Uncle Louie." But the Bishop would prefer more reverence, more decorum. However, he says nothing. At Mass today I did not give the nuns the kiss of peace for fear of the Bishop. Several of the Precious Blood Sisters came with bangs—a slightly different hairdo.

❧

There were three or four copies of *Ave Maria* on the table but I did not get to look at them to see if my statement on draft record burning was there.[34] Nor have I had any repercussions. A letter from Phil Berrigan (Allentown Prison, Pa.) was forwarded from Gethsemani. He does not mind prison life. But demonstrations & draft card burnings are not understood: they help Wallace. Is it possible he may be President? Yes, possible.

❧

LATE AFTERNOON. Rain. Cold. I got home from preaching the Day of Recollection to (most of) the Sisters of the Diocese at Providence Hospital. It was good & I was less tired than I expected. The grey nuns of Kodiak (mostly old—one little young one looking slightly lost & *very* young). The ones at Marian House (various groups—Bishop & I & Frs. [Thomas] Connery & [John] Lunney concelebrated & had dinner there last night). The Precious Blood nuns from Eagle River—my old friends—two Episcopalians with blue veils, two from Copper Center, the Good Shepherd nun from Philadelphia who, it seems, came up on the same plane with me . . . (Could it have been the same one?) and the Providence nuns at the hospital.

⚜

Came home. Bishop's house empty (he is at Palmer, at the parish feast of St. Michael's). I stood in the wet, empty, leaf-covered driveway & watched the seagulls flying by in the rain. I probably won't be able to go to Dillingham tomorrow. Tuesday—day of recollection for the priests & then Wednesday I finally go to California.

⚜

All this flying around Alaska has been paid for by the Bishop.

We had a good talk last evening & he agreed that if I came to Alaska it would be simply to live as a hermit with *no* kind of parish responsibility.

⚜

Yesterday morning—driving in rain up the shore of the channel, past Mendenhall Glacier, outside Juneau. Shrine of St. Therese in rain. Lovely big trees. A good spot—but not for me (would be swamped by people). Juneau is a handsome little town. I could get quite fond of it! Mass in an old church in Douglas. (The churches here are poverty stricken!) Flight out of Juneau on a big jet from Los Angeles—back into the high & prosperous realm above the clouds.

❧

September 30

Light snow in Anchorage on the last day of September.

❧

Flew to Dillingham in a Piper Aztec (two engines) a fast plane that goes high. Bristol Bay area—like Siberia! Miles of tundra. Big winding rivers. At times, lakes are crowded together & shine like bits of broken glass. Or are untidy & complex like the pieces of a jigsaw puzzle.

Two volcanoes: *Iliamna*—graceful, mysterious, feminine, akin to the great Mexican volcanoes. A volcano to which one speaks with reverence, lovely in the distance, standing above the sea of clouds. Lovely near at hand with smaller attendant peaks. *Redoubt* (which surely has another name, a secret & true name) handsome & noble in the distance, but ugly, sinister as you get near it. A brute of a dirty busted mountain that has exploded too often. A bear of a mountain. A dog mountain with steam curling up out of the snow crater. As the plane drew near there was turbulence & we felt the plane might at any moment be suddenly pulled out of its course and hurled against the mountain. As if it would not pull itself away. But finally it did. *Redoubt.* A volcano to which one says nothing. Pictures from the plane.

❧

In Dillingham some time ago (a year or two) the sister of the Orthodox priest went berserk & tore through the Catholic mission with an axe, breaking down one door after another as the Catholic Father retired before her from room to room, calling the State Troopers on various telephones.

❧

Dillingham—grey sky, smelling of snow. Cold wind. Freezing. Brown tundra. Low hemlocks. In the distance, interesting mountains. We flew to them, between them. Brown vacant slopes. A distance somewhat like New Mexico (flat, dark blue line). Another distance with snow covered mountains vanishing into low clouds. Lake Aleknagik speaks to me. A chain of lakes far from everything. Is this it?

❧

Aleknagik.

Nunavaugaluk (a very impressive deserted lake—separated
          mountains).

Akuluktok Peak.

Nuyakuk River (the big river at Dillingham—from Nuyakuk
          Lake).

October 2

BIG BLACK MOUTHS of the jet engines open in silver fog. We bounce high over the Chugach lifting out of Anchorage.

✤

We come up into the sunlight, possibly over Cordova.

✤

"My own journey & life-goal which had colored my dreams since late boyhood was to see the beautiful Princess Fatima and if possible to win her love."

(H. Hesse, *Journey to the East*)

✤

"I met & loved Ninon, known as 'the foreigner' "... She was jealous of Fatima "the princess of my dreams & yet she was probably Fatima herself without knowing it."[35]

✤

Yesterday—Day of Recollection for some 50 priests at P B convent. Almost half of them chaplains, many of these in from "the sites" (missile launching sites etc. in the Aleutians & Far North).

✤

Sister Mary wrote me a very sweet note on the back of a card showing an "Alaskan Sunset." I have not been able to throw it away. Mother Rita Mary gave me a good clock. The incredible generosity of Archbishop Ryan. Tom Connery waited with me for the plane (an hour late). Msgr. [Francis A.] Murphy ended up by cooking a fine steak dinner (we flew to Dillingham together Monday). Tom Connery goes to Dillingham Friday (for 2 weeks).

⚜

"Among the tram ways & banks of Zurich we came upon Noah's Ark guarded by several dogs which all had the same name."[36]

⚜

Perpetual mist grant unto them O Lord. The seatbelt sign is on "Please Fasten your Seatbelts Thank yo!" What is this "Thankyo!"? Is it west? Is it only Alaska?

⚜

Suddenly I hear a steelband I had on tape in the hermitage.

⚜

NINE RULES FOR AIR TRAVEL

1—Get the last window seat in the back, next to the kitchen.
2—Get Bloody Mary when the girls start off with their wagon.
3—Read Hermann Hesse, *Journey to the East*.
4—No use looking out the window. Fog all the way up to 36,000 feet.
5—Get second Bloody Mary when girls come back down aisle.

6—Expect small dinner, racket of which is right beside you (slamming of ice box doors, etc.).

7—Sympathy & admiration for hardworking stewardesses.

8—Cocktail almonds in pocket for Suzanne who is supposed to be at airport in San Francisco—assuming we make some kind of connection in Seattle!

9—"We had brought the magic wave with us. It cleansed everything." (Hesse)[37]

✤

The sky finally opened when we were over British Columbia & all its islands and on the way down into Seattle we flew over at least six big forest fires and a lot of small ones that were nearly out. But the big ones were by no means out and now south of Seattle the whole lower sky is red-brown with the smoke of big distant fires. Volcanoes stand up out of it. Mt. Hood etc.

No connection at Seattle so we stay on this plane, & it will stop at SF.

Title for a possible book *The Fun Diary of My Uncle*—anti-salacious.

✤

October 3

THEN there was Portland (where we were not supposed to be) & the plane filled up & I finished Hermann Hesse & Paul Bowles[38] & looked out at the scarred red flanks of Lassen Peak and as we landed in SF a carton of Pepsi cans broke open & the cans rolled around all over the floor in the back galley & even a little bit forward, under the feet of some sailors.

Embraced wildly by Suzanne in airport. Her little sister Linda was so quiet. And she talked of her music & her ballet & her French (good accent). Then they went home & I slept nine hours in the (expensive) motel.

⚡

Stewardess 1—"When her eyelashes began to fall out I..." (inaudible).
Stewardess 2—"Real ones?"
Stewardess 1—"Yes!"

⚡

This morning the big American Freight went up ahead of us black-smoking in the fog & a big Japanese passenger came down blinking gladly from Asia & then we tugged at ourselves a little with our propellers & then came up here where we are now high over a lake of dirty cotton, in the baby blue sky of California.

I can't remember the last sign I saw down there in that world, but something beautiful like

XAMN RNWY   BFR XING

Epilogue / *The Redwoods*

October 8

MORE THAN A WEEK since I last wrote in this thing. I am now at the Redwoods Monastery. Dawn. Cold, hard frost, & a quiet crow softly cawing outside. It is good to be here.

Last Monday—flew to Dillingham (Alaska) over the volcanoes. A fine wild spot—desolate as Siberia. I like the lakes that are to the north of it. Tuesday, a day of recollection for the priests there. Many chaplains. I spoke mostly of prayer. The Bishop was pleased. Wednesday I flew south to San Francisco . . . Then on Thursday morning I flew to Santa Barbara. Spoke informally at the Center & in the evening met some people at Ferry's.[39]

The Alaskan Letters

These sixteen letters are what survives in the Thomas Merton Studies Center of Thomas Merton's Alaskan correspondence. The letters are mostly "business" ones, reports to his Abbot and details about his travels. They are to four people: Father Flavian Burns, O.C.S.O., Abbot of Gethsemani; Brother Patrick Hart, O.C.S.O., acting-secretary to Merton who was handling his affairs during his absence; Brother Lawrence Gannon, O.C.S.O., Abbot's secretary; and Wilbur Hugh "Ping" Ferry, Director of the Center for the Study of Democratic Institutions in Santa Barbara, California, where Merton was to go for a few days on leaving Alaska. The letters, particularly the "reports" to Abbot Burns, further detail Merton's impressions of Alaska during his stay there.

Sept. 17. 1968

Dear Pat

Hi! Everything was fine in New Mexico—now I'm heading for Alaska.

In New Mexico I stopped at the house of the artist Georgia O'Keeffe. Could you please have someone send her
> *Conjectures*
> *Chuang Tzu*

and whatever *Monks Pond* are available?
> Miss Georgia O'Keeffe
> Abiquiu, N.M. 87510

And please send *Cargo Theology*, along with one or two recent mimeographs, to the monastery (as above)
and—one *Cargo Theology* to
> Fr Xavier Carroll, OFM
> Poor Clares
> 9000 So Kean Av
> Hickory Hills, Ill.
> 60457

Thanks a lot! My best to everyone. Keep well.

> In the Lord,
> Louie

Sept. 18

Dear Pat

I just tried to notarize this but it's nearly impossible with the present form. It has to be signed by someone in Kentucky. I suggest you contact John Ford & have it drawn up in such a way that the *Abbey* transfers the rights & Fr Flavian can sign it. That is the only way. John obviously didn't know I'd gone.

More later. I'm writing this at the Post Office. Alaska—*terrific.*

Best to all
Louie

Monastery of the Precious Blood
Box 1127
Eagle River, Ak. 99577
Sept. 18

Dear Br Lawrence

Many thanks for the mail which arrived yesterday—or rather was given to me at the airport when I arrived. Passport, tickets, all O.K. I'll get Indonesian visa in San Francisco & the rest can wait until I'm over there.

I am doing a workshop with the nuns here—nice little contemplative community in the woods. I live in a trailer nearby. Very good set up. Alaska is just fine.

I enclose a letter from Dom Colomban. He has a friend called Abbe Pierre Lucas who is under the illusion that I have many millionaire friends & can get money from them to help him. Well, he *does* need help. But I'm not the man to get it. I tried Clare Boothe Luce—the only really rich person I know—& she didn't answer.

The only thing I can think of is for the monastery to send him *as many mass stipends* as possible (for priests he is helping—) & perhaps other help too, a regular check or something. Anyway, maybe Br Norbert can think of something. I spoke to him about it once.

My best—thanks for everything—love to all.
Louie

Please tell Br Pat I am trying to get the document for J. Ford notarized today.

Box 1127
Eagle River, Alaska 99577
Sept. 20

Dear Pat

I haven't had much time for letter writing—pretty busy with the nuns to whom I am giving a workshop. The woods are fine & this is great country, really wild, lots of mountains, much solitude.

Could you send some of the recent mimeographs on contemplative life to these nuns? Precious Blood Monastery at the above address. Maybe also Br Richard could send them a copy of *New Seeds of Contemplation* and *Life & Holiness,* also *Faith & Violence* (For free of course).

When the workshop is over I expect to see a lot more of this area & look forward to doing so.

As regards the ms of Fr. Venard — I guess my letter never reached him.

How's everything there? Best wishes to all.

In the Lord
Louie

Alaska
Sept. 24

Dear Pat

Thanks for latest letters & mass stipends. They come in handy—
never know when I will fail to be "met" at airports, have to take
cab etc.

Have finished a workshop with the nuns—pretty good—& have
seen some fabulous wild country. No question that this is the place
for solitude—plus earthquakes, bears etc.—& long dark winters.

More things to send:
(1) *New Seeds of Contemplation—Conjectures of G.B.*
    Praying the Psalms
                    to Rev Segundo Llorente S J
                        Box 79
                        Cordova, Alaska 99574
(2) *Conjectures of G. Bystander*
    Mystics & Zen Masters
                    to Precious Blood Monastery
                        Box 1127
                        Eagle River, Alaska 99577

Am on the move pretty much. Up here you have to go everywhere by plane—there are almost no roads.

My best to everyone. Hope the rumors
are dying down.

In Xt
Louie

43

Anchorage
Sept. 25. 68

Dear Fr Flavian

I am writing this in the Chancery Office while waiting to get my flight to California confirmed. It is an unfamiliar typewriter so I don't guarantee the legibility of what I am writing.

Also it is very good to be away from the typewriter for so long, with the prospect of being away from it still longer. I have had to put off going to California for a couple of days more because I am flying all over the place up here in bush planes and getting a real good idea of what it is all about. That is what I want to report on so far. I already have a good grasp of the situation and will see a great deal more.

There is no question that this place is full of ideal solitude in every form. So far I have seen the Anchorage area which is not so good—relatively crowded, big army bases etc. Southeast of here there is a wild coast going for thousands of miles down to Vancouver, with literally thousands of little islands, most of which would be too remote or savage to live on. But there are many which would be very practical and near some small town that could be reached by boat. Most of these small towns are themselves cut off from the outside world, have no roads anywhere and are reached by plane. The ones I have seen are small fishing villages the size of New Haven. Miles from nowhere, but with a small Catholic population of a few families maybe.

I have also seen the Chugach mountains which are extremely wild and probably too wild to live in mostly. Some of the central area which would be too cold. I am interested in the coast and expect to see a lot more of it in the next few days. The Bishop and clergy here are extremely generous and encouraging and the people are simple frontier types. I think Alaska would be the best place in the US for a hermitage.

Everything else is going well. I'll write again when I have seen more. I am in great shape (climbed a 2000 foot mountain last Sunday). The place is crawling with bears, some of which are dangerous others not. Yesterday the bush pilot waS SKIDDING ALONG THE FLANKS OF HIGH MOUNTAINS (that got capitalized by mistake, no emphasis intended) to find bear and mountain goats. In every respect I am finding this trip most helpful and encouraging. I am sure that if nothing else comes up there will be hundreds of places in Alaska and many to help us make good use of them if we wish.

Please keep up the prayers, my best wishes to all,
My warmest regards in Christ
Louie

Anchorage
Sept. 25. 1968

Dear Ping

I am due to arrive in Santa Barbara on United flight 899 at 10 a.m. October 3rd. All set. The country here is *marvelous*— never seen the like—flying all around in bush planes. This is a wild grand & exciting country.

More soon,
Tom Merton

Anchorage
Sept. 26. 68

Dear Fr Flavian

Yesterday I wrote in a big hurry on a most unfamiliar typewriter. This is still not the kind of machine I am used to but there is more time and I can run it better. So I thought I'd better try to give you a good report on what has been going on and what the situation is as I see it so far.

1. I have now seen quite a lot of the area within a five hundred mile radius of Anchorage. This includes a lot of wild mountains, a mountain range bigger than the Swiss Alps, another range where the highest mountain on this continent is found, a rugged coast-line with thousands of isolated bays and islands and glaciers, with a few fishing villages that can only be reached by air or by a very long boat trip. I have also seen a vast central valley with miles of nothing, millions of small lakes, canyons etc., and a few settlements, roads etc. This area is very cold in winter. The coast line is less cold but very rainy. In fact today I am supposed to go down to Juneau and a lot of the planes are grounded down that way because of torrential rains. However at Juneau there is an old chapel and some cabins originally built as a retreat center by an earlier bishop and now abandoned. It may be a possibility but I think it is too near Juneau which (though not much bigger and perhaps smaller than Bardstown) is the state capital.

2. I have yet to see and explore more of those bays and islands in SE Alaska and have a hunch that near a half-breed village of fishing people called Yakutat (totally isolated) I might find a good spot.

47

I have also to see the western part of Alaska which is vast and empty without even mountains and forests, and is a place where priests are sent when they are in disgrace as a punishment—it is so lonely. This too might be just ideal.

3. The Bishop is extremely generous and good. He is very interested in having contemplatives here, and very happy that I might possibly be a hermit here. I am almost certain that I would have to at least say Mass on Sundays for a few families in some isolated place, and nothing much more than that would be involved, if I protected firmly my solitude. (Otherwise I feel he'd have me up in Anchorage giving conferences to priests and nuns.) He has meanwhile gone out of his way to get me around, chartered bush planes for me and really I have explored the place very thoroughly (though not of course the far north).

4. My feeling at present is that Alaska is certainly the ideal place for solitude and the hermit life. In fact it is full of people who are in reality living as hermits. Men who have gone far out into the wilderness with a stack of books and who get themselves a homestead, cut wood, read, and stay away from everyone, living on moose, fish, caribou etc. I don't plan it that way. But it gives you a good idea of the character of the place. There is also an old Russian Orthodox monk who has lived for years as a hermit off Kodiak Island and in fact before him there was a Staretz there who is venerated as a saint, so religious hermits are nothing new here. Unfortunately I was not able to get to Kodiak and this old monk is now sick anyway but I hope to meet him someday before he dies.

In conclusion, though I am not in a position to decide anything yet, I believe that if nowhere else there is certainly real solitude in Alaska and that it would be very easy (in spite of obvious problems, weather, bears, and all that) to settle here. The priests and people would welcome a hermit. They are all good simple people, not yet caught up in the mess of problems which are found in the

States. I think that unless something very definite comes up to change things, this would be the obvious place to settle for real solitude in the United States. Also, apart from that, I think that it is a place where God is calling some to solitude. The Bishop himself is very definite about wanting contemplatives and a real contemplative life here, and would be greatly pleased to have me stay. He and everyone I have met make this very clear. I can't say with certitude that I think I am called to be a hermit here, but I do believe it is a very real possibility and that I must keep it in mind and look into it further and perhaps make a decision on my return from Asia.

As to the material problems, people are very resourceful in handling them and very cooperative with one another so that when anyone is in trouble they will always come to his assistance by plane etc. There is no unusual risk or danger when this is taken into consideration. As to the cold, people who have experience of different parts of the States assure me that it would not be any worse than the Genesee along the coast here, and less bad than Montana, the Dakotas etc.

I guess that covers it so far. It has been wonderful here and I still have a lot more to see that sounds very interesting. I feel that I haven't seen the best of it yet. Last Sunday I climbed a small mountain & really had a workout. My health seems better up here and the allergies that bothered me down there are much less troublesome here. Drop me a line if you get a chance. Love to all.

My very best, in the Lord,
Louie

Anchorage
Sept. 26

Dear Pat:

Thanks for the latest mail, including the New Guinea archbishop etc. Maybe you could reply to Bishop [Joseph Matthew] Breitenbeck, and suggest Mother Myriam [Dardene] ought to attend the meeting he mentions. She would be a "must" in my opinion.

The Syracuse Library thing I sent to J. Laughlin. J will know what to do.

I want to enclose a few postcards and notes for some of the gang with this, and may mail it from Juneau where I am flying with the Bishop today—though bad weather has a lot of flights delayed or cancelled. One of the things that can easily happen here is that you wait around half a day or more and eventually get stranded in some lost fishing village for a couple of days. Hasn't happened to me yet, but maybe . . . Anyway everyone here is very nice and I have been all over the place in bush planes, really wild country and just terrific from every point of view. The mountains have got the Alps beat a mile. This is utterly unique. Lots of live volcanoes too.

Could you please get from Fr Eudes [Bamberger] a supply of DONNATAL tablets and send them to me at Redwoods?

My trip to Cal has been delayed slightly and I will be at Santa Barbara until Oct. 4, so you can send stuff that will reach me there until that date. Then Redwoods.

This is all very fine here but I am getting impatient for India. That is the real purpose of the trip. Keep up the prayers. There are so many things involved in dialog with Asian peoples and I really need a special charism—to say the least. And it is so important.

Give my regards to all the gang and I hope there are not too many crazy rumors. Keep telling everyone that I am a monk of Gethsemani and intend to remain one all my days—only I just happen to be out of the monastery, just as some have been absent to go to Rome etc.

There is a lady here to whom I promised a copy of *Selected Poems*. If I remember, I'll enclose her card, I don't have it here. Oh, here is also the letter of Rev Mr. [Donald] Allchin (correct title for Anglican priest). Tell him about Basil [Pennington]'s project to perhaps print *Climate*. But if he wants to mimeograph it also, he can do so, but in that case we should send him the new script which Cecilia Wilma is typing, when we get it—I don't know. Leave decision to him. (It's in England and so would not interfere with printing project.)

Everything and everyone just fine here. A whole new sense of Church and of community out here on the frontier. It is very striking. The charity is quite unusual—and people are still solid and simple Catholics without too many of the new complicated problems. Refreshing.

Best always, love to all,
Louie

Anchorage
Sept. 26

Dear Br Lawrence

I flew over this [Portage Glacier] in a small plane the other day.
There are hundreds like it all over the place & many beautiful
islands. Alaska is certainly the most beautiful part of America &
the people are very nice too. However I'm anxious to get going
to Asia. Keep well!

Blessings
Louie

Anchorage
Sept. 26. 1968

Dear Ping

Your note of the 24 just reached me here in the Chancery Office of the Archdiocese of Anchorage where I am wrestling with the mysteries of an electric typewriter. Since the Archbishop is using to the full my potential for shooting off my crazy (yeeow what a word) mouth I see no reason why I shd not seek to pick up a shilling or even a half crown in Santa Claus Barbarossa. The only stipulation would be no immediate press publicity. I can perhaps think up material for a "paper" on something—at least something to do with what I am about to do in Asia. In fact probably the best thing would be to present some informal ideas as to how everything looks about the trip, now, and then a report of how it went when I get back. Before and after, so to speak. It could be quite interesting. The extra day would give me time to lie around and have a much needed rest as I have been moving pretty fast over this great country, bush planes at all hours of day and night, glacier tundra, bear wallow and moose run, aND (nuts) will also have to talk again to many nunnies and good fathers. As I wrote yesterday I plan to sail into Santa Barbara on United Fl. 899 from San Francisco on the morning of October 3, 10 o'clock.

This would give me practically two days in yr villa, and as I said before I am going to be very anxious to lie around and read and think a bit. There will also be time to meet the folks and so on. If our exploration of Cal. is a bit shorter it won't affect much my original purpose because I have found enough lonely spots here in AZlaska (zow that's a grand word) to last any hermit until

53

judgement day. It is quite possible that if and whenever I get back from Asia I may end up here. Local Bishop xtrelely (extremely) friendly and gene rous (generous) and everybody very helpful. Lots of little lost islands and spots like fishing villages with two Catlick families who'd be glad to have Mass on Sundays, wonderful lost towns with no road to them only reachable by plane or boat, places turned upside down by tidal wave and earthquake and moved to another spot etc. The mountains are the finest I have ever seen anywhere. It is GREAT land. Today off to Juneau and SE Alaska and then back to Anchorage for the nunnies. Before I go on Wed I will get a look at the west end down toward the Aleutians where there is a lost lake amid tundra that sounds fab. (Near the usual fishing village for food.) Have eaten moose but not yet bear.

Could run on forever. Plans excellent. Will hold forth Oct 4 and glad of any small shillings to take to farthest Ind. See you Oct 3 at Santa B.

Best of everything to all. Hope Rabbi Vedanta's books arrived not to mention pants from New Mexico.

Salud.
Tom

Sept. 27

Dear Pat

Here is the address of Mrs Johnstone to whom *Selected Poems* & *Raids on the Unspeakable* should be sent. Thanks.

Did not make it to Juneau yesterday—due to bad flying weather. Trying again today.

Best
Louie

Anchorage
Sept. 30

Dear Pat

I'm still in Alaska—but leaving day after tomorrow. Could the bookstore please send *Sign of Jonas* (paper) to

Frank Ryman
Yakutat
Alaska 99689

Got to Juneau a day late—flying through high mountains in fog & snow clouds is an interesting experience! Today I am to fly to a place 400 miles west & see a different aspect of Alaska. The Bishop is paying for all this—he is very gracious! I still think this is a wonderful place & the people are great.

Could you please send me a couple of copies of the essay I wrote on R. Barthes—at Redwoods?

Many thanks—best wishes to everyone.

In Xto
Louie

It snowed here yesterday (Sept 29)!

Anchorage
~~Sept. 30~~   Oct. 1

Dear Bro Lawrence

Here is a refund slip on a flight which I changed. I am flying from here to San Francisco tomorrow, will spend the night there & go to Santa Barbara the next day. My California stay will be shortened but I have had a busy time here & the Bishop has been flying me all over Southern Alaska. I know the South well by now—but haven't seen the Far North. It is already snowing in the "South." The Jesuit missionaries, alone in Eskimo villages a thousand miles north of here, are *real* solitaries!!

Have managed to raise a little money here & I'm going out richer than I came in, so there is no financial problem—yet.

I hope all is well at Gethsemani. Love to all.

In Xt.
Louie

Anchorage — Alaska
Oct. 1. 1968

Dear Fr Flavian

I thought you'd like to see some photos of one of the best places I have found. These are pictures of a lake & a bay near Cordova, Alaska—a small fishing village that can be reached only by plane. Completely isolated—already a parish priest there so no obligation to take care of anyone—one could live five or six miles out of town & be very quiet. Of course there are a few bears, but I am told they are not grizzlies—i.e. they won't normally attack you.

I had a very frank talk with the Bishop & he agreed perfectly that I would not be asked to do any parish work of any kind—the only request would be to help priests by spiritual direction if they wanted to come all the way down there to see me. It is about 300 miles or more from Anchorage.

As I said before I have made no commitments, but I do feel that I should consider seriously the many generous offers of small parcels of land or of rights to live on land etc that have been made. It would be folly for me not to consider Alaska as one of the best possibilities for a true solitary life & I hope I can return here when I am through in Asia. The Bishop has been very generous & the people have been fine. They would be entranced if you wanted to send a small group but I did not encourage them to hope. You ought to see this country some time!

I fly to California tomorrow.
All my best, in Xto,
br m Louis

Anchorage
Oct. 2

Dear Pat

I'm leaving today after two very fruitful weeks. Expect to find some mail in Santa Barbara tomorrow.

Meanwhile—more things to send:

1) To Fr. Richard O'Dea
       c/o Archbishop Ryan   Box 2239   Anchorage
  Monks Pond
  Articles on Joyce, Barthes, & if possible, the one on Faulkner
  (*Baptism in Wilderness*) (Bro Martin shd have it!) (?)

2) To Rose Golik   c/o Archbishop
  A Thomas Merton Reader

I hope I am not having too many books sent out. All these people have been very generous.

No time for more—will write from California.

All my best—in Xto.
Louie

Notes

Introduction

1. Monica Furlong allots one line to the Alaskan trip: "[He] made visits to Alaska with the help of the bishop." (*Merton: a Biography*, p. 319). Jim Forest does not even mention these trips as such—Merton was in California "on his way to Asia." (*Thomas Merton: a Pictorial Biography*, p. 93). Deba Patnaik in his "Chronology" in *Geography of Holiness* says, in error, that Merton "[started] a workshop for nuns at Yakutat, Alaska." He not only started it, but finished it, and, of course, the workshop was at the Monastery of the Precious Blood in Eagle River, *not* in Yakutat which Merton found wild and isolated. The documentary, *Merton: a Film Biography*, produced by Paul Wilkes and Audrey L. Glynn, has nearly one-quarter of its length devoted to the Asian trip, but nothing to his earlier travels.

2. Thomas Merton Studies Center, Bellarmine College, *Notebook* #40, p. 105.

3. Alexander Lipski claims in his book, *Thomas Merton and Asia: His Quest for Utopia* (Kalamazoo, Michigan: Cistercian Publications, 1983), that Asia was "uppermost in Merton's mind."

4. *See* Robert E. Daggy, "Journey to Publication: Bringing *Woods, Shore, Desert* into Print," *Merton Seasonal* 8 (Summer 1983): no. 2, pp. 2–3.

5. Patrick Hart, "Foreword." In *Woods, Shore, Desert: a Notebook, May 1968* (Santa Fe: Museum of New Mexico Press, 1983): p. viii.

6. Merton traveled in June 1956 to Collegeville, Minnesota, for a liturgical conference and in June 1964 to New York City to confer with D. T. Suzuki.

7. Thomas Merton Studies Center, Bellarmine College, *Notebook* #14, unpaged.

8. Thomas Merton Studies Center, "Transcript of Remarks at Closed Session, Center for the Study of Democratic Institutions, Santa Barbara, October 3, 1968": p. 4.

9. "September Circular Letter to Friends," *The Asian Journal of Thomas Merton* (New York: New Directions, 1973): pp. 295-296.

10. Monica Furlong, *Merton: a Biography* (San Francisco: Harper & Row, 1980): p. 319.

11. Lipski, op. cit., *passim*.

12. "Transcript of Remarks at Closed Session . . .": p. 2.

The Alaskan Journal

1. The Embassy Club: A popular supper club on Shelbyville Road in St. Matthews, Kentucky, an eastern suburb of Louisville.

2. Archbishop of Anchorage: John Joseph Thomas Ryan (1913–   ), Archbishop of Anchorage 1966–1975; appointed Titular Archbishop of Gabi and Co-adjutor to the Military Vicar in 1975.

3. The Vicar General: Monsignor George E. Gallant.

4. *Bardo Thödöl: The Tibetan Book of the Dead; or, the After-Death Experiences on the BARDO Plane, according to Lama Kazi Dawa-Sandup's English Rendering;* compiled and edited by Walter Yeeling Evans-Wentz (Oxford: Oxford University Press, 1960). This passage is excerpted and paraphrased from p. 104. Merton was reading *The Tibetan Book of the Dead* on the airplane, having already recorded some passages during his flights to and from New Mexico. He had read Evans-Wentz's editions of *Tibetan Yoga and Secret Doctrines* (London, 1968) and *Tibet's Great Yogi, Milarepa* (London, 1951). He had planned to include a 1936 lecture delivered by Evans-Wentz in Calcutta, "The Tibetan Science of Death," in his "little magazine" *Monks Pond*, but omitted it from the final issue.

5. From *The Tibetan Book of the Dead*: p. 121.

6. Sangsara: A term which refers to the phenomenal universe itself, its opposite being *Nirvana*.

7. Drawn from *The Tibetan Book of the Dead*: p. 125. Lokas: Worlds.

8. Lawrence Durrell and Henry Miller, *A Private Correspondence*, edited by George Wilkes (New York: E. P. Dutton, 1963).

62

9. Ron Seitz: (1935–   ), poet, friend and protégé of Merton's; his poetry was included in *Monks Pond*; now a Professor of English at Bellarmine College in Louisville; author of articles on Merton; his poem "To Tom Gone" was included in *A Merton Concelebration*; ed. Deba Prasad Patnaik (Notre Dame, Indiana: Ave Maria Press, 1981): p. 63.

10. Merton was particularly fond of James Joyce and had written three articles on him, two of them specifically on *Ulysses*: "Correspondence: A Note on Joyce's *Ulysses*," *Sewanee Review* 76 (Autumn 1968): no. 4, p. 694; "News of the Joyce Industry," *Sewanee Review* 77 (Summer 1969): no. 3, pp. 543–554 [later included in *The Literary Essays of Thomas Merton* (1982): pp. 12–22]; "Peace and Revolution: a Footnote from *Ulysses*," *Peace* 3 (Fall–Winter 1968–1969): pp. 4–10 [also included in *Thomas Merton on Peace* (1971): pp. 70–75 and in *The Literary Essays of Thomas Merton* (1982): pp. 23–28].

11. From *The Tibetan Book of the Dead*: p. 127.

12. From *The Tibetan Book of the Dead*: p. 128.

13. From *The Tibetan Book of the Dead*: pp. 131–132.

14. This passage is paraphrased from *The Tibetan Book of the Dead*: p. 128.

15. From *The Tibetan Book of the Dead*: p. 129.

16. Fr. Xavier: Father Xavier Carroll, O.F.M.

17. From *The Tibetan Book of the Dead*: p. 129.

18. Rev. Segundo Llorente, S.J.: priest at Cordova, Alaska, and one of Merton's hosts.

19. George Corley Wallace: (1919–   ), Governor of Alabama 1963–1966 and 1971–1979; candidate for President in 1968 on the American Independent Party Ticket; his running-mate was General Curtis LeMay.

20. General Curtis Erving LeMay: (1906–   ), Chief of Staff, U.S. Air Force 1961–1964; Candidate for Vice-President with George Wallace in 1968 on the American Independent Party Ticket; opposed bombing halt and urged maintenance of military strength and position in Vietnam; went to Vietnam for Wallace on fact-finding tour October 16 to 19; was in Alaska on his way to Vietnam.

21. Nicholas Joseph Begich: (1932–1972), Superintendent of Schools, Fort Richardson, Alaska 1963–1968; Member, Alaska Senate 1963–1971; U.S. Congressman from Alaska 1971–1972.

22. Rama Krishna: Ramakrishna Parahamsa (1834–1886), Hindu ascetic and mystic, open to other forms of religious expression, he meditated for a time as a Christian and as a Muslim, reaching the conclusion that "all religions are one"; his disciples introduced a new element of social service into Hinduism.

23. Fr. Flavian, Bros. Maurice, Patrick: Father Flavian Burns, Abbot of Gethsemani 1968–1973; Brother Maurice Flood; Brother Patrick Hart (1925–), Merton's "secretary" during his absence.

24. O'Callaghan's: Frank and Thomasine [Tommie] O'Callaghan; Merton had often stayed at their home in Louisville [See: Tommie O'Callaghan, "From Lamb Chops to Peanut Butter," *St. Anthony Messenger* 86 (December 1978): no. 7, p. 37]; Tommie O'Callaghan was named by Merton as one of the original trustees of the Merton Legacy Trust and she has served in that capacity since 1968.

25. Dan Walsh: Daniel C. Walsh (1907–1975), Merton's teacher at Columbia; long-time friend and mentor [See: Anthony Distefano, "Dan Walsh's Influence on the Spirituality of Thomas Merton," *Merton Seasonal* 5 (Late Summer 1979): no. 2, pp. 4–13].

26. St. Bonaventure Friary: Bonaventure Hall on the Bellarmine College campus in Louisville; in 1968 it housed Franciscan teachers and professors; later used as a residence for diocesan seminarians; since 1976 it has housed the Thomas Merton Studies Center and has been a Conference Center for seminars, retreats, etc.

27. Tom Carlyle: *See* Merton's lengthy discussion of Carlyle, whom he liked very much, in his Alaskan conference "Community, Politics, and Contemplation," *Sisters Today* 42 (January 1971): no. 5, p. 243.

28. Merton was reading and quoting from *Vladimir Lossky* (1903–1958), *A l'Image et a la Ressemblance de Dieu* (Paris: Aubion-Montaigne, 1967): p. 183.

29. Walter J. Hickel: Governor of Alaska 1966–1969; U.S. Secretary of the Interior 1969–1970; Hickel's appointment to the Interior Department by Richard M. Nixon was opposed by conservationists because of his long-standing business association with the oil industry. Hickel sent a publicized

letter to Nixon in May 1970 accusing the administration of being "insensitive" to students and young people and urging that "youth in its protest [against the Vietnamese War] must be heard." Nixon dismissed Hickel on November 25, 1970, stating that their relationship lacked "essential elements of mutual confidence."

30. Suzanne B.: Suzanne Butorovich, a young girl in San Francisco, who initiated a correspondence with Merton; in their letters they discussed Bob Dylan, the Beatles, and the hippie movement; Merton signed himself as "Hippie Hermit" in some of his letters to her.

31. Dermot O'Flanagan: (1901–1973), Bishop of Juneau 1951–1968.

32. Ernest Gruening: (1887–1974), Governor of Alaska Territory 1939–1953; Senator from Alaska 1959–1969.

33. Fr. Manske: Monsignor James I. Manske, Vicar General of the Diocese of Juneau.

34. The article was titled "Non-violence does not—cannot—mean passivity," *Ave Maria* 108 (7 September 1968): no. 8, pp. 9–10. It was included as "Note for *Ave Maria*" in *Thomas Merton on Peace* (1971): pp. 231–233.

35. From Hermann Hesse, *The Journey to the East*; translated from the German by Hilda Rosner (New York: Farrar, Straus & Giroux, 1961): p. 24.

36. From *The Journey to the East*: p. 28.

37. From *The Journey to the East*: pp. 9–10.

38. Paul Frederic Bowles: (1910–   ), American writer, poet, novelist, translator, composer and expatriate, living in Tangier, Morocco. It is not clear what Merton was reading of Bowles' since none of his writings survived among Merton's books, but it may have been his translation from the Moghrabi of Mohammed Mrabet's *Love with a Few Hairs* (New York: P. Owen, 1967). New Directions had reprinted Bowles' *The Sheltering Sky* in 1967 and Black Sparrow Press published a collection of poems, *Scenes*, in 1968.

39. W[ilbur] H[ugh] "Ping" Ferry: (1910–   ), then Director of the Center for the Study of Democratic Institutions at Santa Barbara, California; editor of *Letters from Tom* (Scarsdale, New York: Fort Hill Press, 1984); See pages 46 and 53 for Merton's letters to Ferry from Alaska.

Part Two
The Alaskan Conferences

The Alaskan Conferences

Thomas Merton gave several conferences or talks during his stay in Alaska. From September 18 to September 21, he directed a Workshop for the Sisters of the Monastery of the Precious Blood in Eagle River, north of Anchorage. On Sunday, September 29, he preached a Day of Recollection for Sisters of the Diocese at Providence Hospital in Anchorage and on Tuesday, October 1, he conducted a similar Day of Recollection for Priests at the Monastery of the Precious Blood. Tapes of these conferences were returned to the Abbey of Gethsemani and are now on file at the Thomas Merton Studies Center, Bellarmine College. The first seven conferences were transcribed by Brother Patrick Hart and edited by Naomi Burton Stone for publication in *Sisters Today*. Some additional editing has been done by Robert E. Daggy. The Day of Recollection for Priests was taped by Father Bartholomew Egan, C.S.Sp., and transcribed by Father Brian Cogan, C.S.Sp., and published in *The Priest*.

This Is God's Work

We need to remind ourselves that what we are doing is not a human action; it is divine. This is God's work, not our work. We must be very conscious of that fact because today, in the midst of Church renewal, people are too often carried away by the merely human side of what is to be done, and they concentrate too much on their own work, their own efforts, and even their own desires, fancies, and inclinations. All these things are good, but they are secondary, and what is secondary has to remain in second place. What is first is God's work, God's Spirit, and especially is this true in the contemplative life. As contemplatives we are never going to get anywhere unless we realize ourselves that we are completely in God's hands. This realization is much more important in the contemplative life than in any other because, for one thing, the contemplative life reaches far beyond the range of mere human endeavor which exists in the active life.

I use the term "contemplative life," which is a difficult term. Everything we are dealing with is difficult, and we are going to have to make our meaning quite clear. The main point is the action of God's grace in our life. What is important, then, is for us to think about our work and our vocation with a special kind of mental attitude or climate to which we ought always to return, a climate of inner peace and trust rather than a climate of tension and agitation.

It is terribly important that everything we do should be done in a ground of peace within us, rather than in a ground of contention. So much that goes on now in Church renewal tends to develop in an atmosphere of conflict where people are too keyed-up about what is right and what is wrong and are trying to prove that they are right and somebody else is wrong. This is not God's way. Naturally this conflict is bound to arise once in a while, but we must always have this deeper ground of peace and confidence and trust, and we should be aware of it, feel it.

"Feeling" used to be a bad word, and certainly there is a lot of "feeling" we don't need to feel, but we do want to experience this inner peace, this deep peace, and return to it. When that peace is disturbed and upset, STOP! Don't push, don't be too anxious to go ahead when peace is not present. Wait until God's time. This is the general atmosphere that I think it is so important to remember when we are talking about renewal of the contemplative life, and really it is easy to return to that atmosphere all the time. When things get difficult, mixed-up and tense, then drop them and get back to the center of peace. God's work in us is a very, very deep call which is heard in silence in the deepest part of our being. The renewal of the contemplative life is purely and simply an arrangement of our life in such a way that we can respond to this call easily and simply; there is nothing else to it.

The renewal of the contemplative life, therefore, should be first of all a kind of simplification, for which I think you are already aiming. This deep call is very delicate and very personal, and in the depths of our hearts it is really a two-fold call. First of all, it is a call to intimacy with God and to the contemplative life. It always has been. It is also a call to renew the contemplative life or the monastic life, in terms of the present world and the people of the world today as well as in terms of the new relationship to the world.

There are two things that God is asking of us, but they are really one, and that is that we simply be men and women of prayer, people who live close to God, people for whom God is everything and for whom God is enough, God is sufficient. That is the root of peace. We have that peace when God is all we seek. When we start seeking something besides Him, we lose it. That is His call to us—simply to be people who are content to live close to Him and to renew the kind of life in which this closeness is felt and experienced.

Now in addition to this call there is the promise and the covenant. The contemplative life is a covenanted life, as is all Christian life. We have made an agreement with God, an agreement to trust His promise. That is what the covenant is, as God said to Abraham. He called Abraham out of his land: leave your people, leave your father's house, and come to the land I will show you. This is the prototype of all vocations—there is a call and a promise. The covenant consists in listening to the call and believing the promise, and always listening and always believing. That is what we have covenanted. We have not covenanted to give God any great work. We have simply promised that we will listen and that we will believe His promise, and this is terribly important in our life.

If our life loses this sense that God has promised everything to us and that His promise cannot fail, then we are disturbed or upset, running around from pillar to post. But God has said that if we will be quiet and will trust Him and live in peace and not in turmoil and not get too involved in anything that takes us too far away from Him, then He will do the rest. He will be close to us, and He will work through us and save souls through us. We need not worry about it—He is going to do it, and once again this returns us to an atmosphere of peace.

Perhaps this preamble will serve to situate us where we are and to help us know where we stand in relation to what is happening elsewhere. We hear about monastic life in the cities, for instance. What is in it for you? What are you to think about these things? As I say, basically the real touchstone is: how does it affect peace? How does it affect the simplicity, peace and trust, and the covenant and the promise with God?

What we have to consider first is that we are called to the contemplative life in a time when it was never more necessary. Stop and think what it means that a few people are called to this specific kind of peace in a world in which there is no such peace—in a world in which peace is almost impossible. It is a great responsibility, a great challenge, and a beautiful vocation and favor of God. We stop and ask ourselves, "Why did He pick us out?" Well, He did; that's all. And we are called to keep alive a little flame of peace and awareness and love in a world where it is very difficult for it to be kept alive.

Never has the world been so violent and in many respects so insane, and so given to pressure and agitation and conflict. Although men have made brilliant technological advances, they cannot handle them or use them for good. They even seem to turn against man's good. In such a society there have to be specialists in inner peace and love. It is not that the society is bad or wrong but that it is extremely complicated and fast-moving, and there is a tendency to get confused in it. The key word in this regard is the word "alienation."

What is alienation, and what is an alienated person, and what are the results of alienation? Alienation is the psychological condition of somebody who is never allowed to be fully himself. For example, in the social order a slave is an alienated person because he does not belong to himself. His work is not his own. There is no real personal meaning to his life, because everything he does belongs to some-body else. Anything can be taken away at any moment.

Transfer that obvious example to a person who is never able to be himself because he is always dominated by somebody else's ideas or somebody else's tastes or somebody else's saying that this is the way to act and this is the way to see things. We live in a society in which many people are alienated in that sense without realizing it. Their choices are made for them, they don't really have ideas and desires of their own; they simply repeat what has been told them. And yet they think that they are making free choices, and to some extent maybe they are.

What happens to a person in this condition is that, without real-izing it, he does not have any real respect for himself. He thinks that he has ideas and he thinks he is doing what he freely wants to do, but actually he is being pushed around, and this results in a sort of resentment, which in turn leads to hatred and violence under a cover of respectability. This is the problem of our world, psycholo-gists tell us. People feel inner tensions and violence and hatred, and they are ready to explode at any moment because they don't really belong to themselves.

Contemplatives are people who escape this alienation. A contem-plative is someone who has a direct relationship with God in the depths of his heart and who speaks to God. When I was in New Mexico someone showed me a manuscript written by an early Spanish teacher in New Mexico. It was a little book about the Chris-tian education of children. It had all sorts of curious things in it, including a lot of information on how to write letters; how to write the first letter if you are courting somebody. There is a whole list of useful things for ordinary life. But the beginning of the book is a chapter on general principles. Why educate people? What are people? It is written in an old-fashioned devotional style and is very beautiful—a kind of dialogue with God.

What this author brings out is that man should bow down to no one but God. Man is the son of God; he is in a direct relationship with his Father, and when people break into this relationship, getting in between God and man and trying to take away his freedom, an unhealthy situation results. The basic principle of education is to teach people to speak to God as their Father and to bow down to no one but God—a very deep Biblical principle. This is really what the prohibition of idolatry means—"Thou shalt have no other god but me." This is the principle of freedom and the principle of Christian dignity and also the principle of the contemplative life. When you think about what happens if our life is really dedicated to something other than God, then we are first of all alienated, and in a certain sense we are worshipping an idol. We are giving our total allegiance to something that is unreal, something artificial that is not the ultimate reality. That again is the meaning of alienation.

There is a strong passage from Saint John's Gospel where our Lord is talking about freedom. It is in chapter eight where he is arguing with the Pharisees, a really tense, fighting chapter. He said, "If you make my word your home you will indeed be my disciples, you will learn the truth and the truth will make you free" (8:31–32). This is the contemplative life—listening to the Word, making our home in the Word, dwelling in the Word, and being a disciple of the Lord. And the truth will make us free. This relationship to God through the Word of Jesus makes us free because it does not merely give us political liberation, it gives us the Holy Spirit, "the Spirit of freedom," the Spirit of response and sonship. The whole basic meaning of it is in the Holy Spirit.

In that sense we are Pentecostals without necessarily having all

the Pentecostal trimmings. The foundation of our life is that the
Spirit is given and that we are led by the Spirit. Our life should flow
from the presence of the Spirit in us, from the freedom of the Spirit
in us. "They answered, 'We are descended from Abraham and we
have never been the slaves of anyone. What do you mean, "You
will be made free"?' " (8:33f.). They didn't know that they were
slaves. The Pharisees were actually the slaves of their own system,
but they didn't know it. And Jesus replied, "I tell you most solemnly,
everyone who commits sin is a slave. Now the slave's place in the
house is not assured, but the son's place is assured. So if the Son
makes you free, you will be free indeed. I know that you are descended from Abraham, but in spite of that you want to kill me
because nothing I say has penetrated into you. What I, for my part,
speak of is what I have seen with my Father. But you, you put into
action the lessons learned from your father." Our Lord is emphasizing the conflict. Where there is this simplicity, peace, and humility
it is attacked. Without translating this rather strong section into
present terms, you do find people who resent this sort of freedom
existing in the world and being expressed in little contemplative
communities, given to prayer and inner freedom and not dominated by the alienated forces of society. They make a lot of noise
attacking this way of life. They want to stop it and get everybody
into the machine. They do not want to let us be ourselves. But we
have a right to be ourselves as they have the right to be themselves.

"They repeated, 'Our father is Abraham.' Jesus said to them, 'If
you were Abraham's children you would do as Abraham did. As it is,
you want to kill me when I tell the truth as I have learned it from
God; that is not what Abraham did. What you are doing is what
your father does' " (8:39). Our Lord emphasizes the truth that this
is the root of our separation from the world. It isn't that the world

is necessarily evil, but built into it are certain processes which tend to stamp out the life of God and the light of God and the Word of God. So we have to face the fact that to preserve our peace we have to know how to fight.

We are in the middle, called to peace and love and simplicity, called to this spirit of freedom which we learn to experience in a life of prayer. Somehow we have to learn to be guided by the Holy Spirit toward this freedom which can hardly be defined. And at the same time we are surrounded by conflict and by criticism. The attack on contemplatives is that they are not Christian, the contemplative life is not Christian, it is unchristian.

What does this mean? What is the history of the argument? There is nothing about contemplation as such in the Bible. Contemplation is a Greek term, a Platonic term. It reflects a certain Platonic, Greek culture and even a kind of experience which is marginal for a Christian, our critics say. And furthermore, if you push this experience too far you become subjective, involved in yourself—introverted, introspective—and it is unhealthy and it is selfish.

These are some of the arguments, and when we hear them we get fighting mad because we know they are wrong. But it is very hard to say how and where they are wrong and how and where they are beside the point. When you say Platonic contemplation, you are talking about something quite different from Christian contemplation. I think I know by experience that there is a great deal of difference between Platonic contemplation, which is intellectual and philosophical and metaphysical, and the fulfillment of experience in Christian prayer. The Platonic approach is intellectual, a very good experience—perhaps not an experience so much as an understanding of the highest principles. But this has very little to do with the heart, and if it does it is somewhat subjective. But this does not represent the Christian experience at all, the Christian experience of sonship, the Christian experience of being risen with Christ, the Christian experience of having received the Spirit. This is totally different, the Christian experience of Christ living in our hearts. To confuse that issue is really dangerous. The only reason that our critics can do so is because they don't know what Christian contemplation really is. Maybe the term "contemplation" is unfortunate, I don't know. Maybe we should not be using it. But Dom Leclercq, the Benedictine scholar and probably one of the best theologians of our time, uses the term with full force. He says, "Let's talk about the contemplative life," and I will go along with that.

There is another argument against contemplatives—that we are Manichaeans and we despise creation. This is ridiculous. But we have to face the fact that such things are said. What was the basis of the Manichaean accusation? Well, in the old days there were many practices in the cloister that tended to imply it. Take, for example, the question of friendship. You must never be too friendly with any one person. All friendship was wrong, and you had to have an equal love for everybody. But this is not really human because you are bound to love some people more than others, and it should not worry you.

There is another distinction, the distinction between the prophetic and the contemplative way of prayer, which was devised by a Protestant theologian called Heiler. The distinction is good, but it is oversimplified. The prophetic way of prayer is a Biblical, time–history oriented view in which we see salvation history at work. The contemplative way of prayer is thought to be more static and is the presence of God here and now.

But you should not worry about all these things. What really matters is that God is here and now and loves us and dwells within us and we are called to realize this. The contemplative life, as we are using the term, is the full realization of the mystery of Christ. It is the realization of what the mystery of Christ means in my own life and in the life of my community, and realization means a realizing love, a love which is understanding.

Prayer, Personalism, and the Spirit

Sometimes I don't think we realize that we have the choice of many approaches to prayer. It isn't a question of there being one right way to pray, or one right answer to the question of prayer, and we should be perfectly free to explore all sorts of avenues and ways of prayer. As you may know, I am personally very much interested in Asian methods of prayer—how they pray and how they meditate because they are, and always have been, deeply involved in meditation.

We may think of ourselves as people who know how to meditate, but the Western Church doesn't really know what meditation is. And, of course, when I say "meditation" I do not mean mental prayer. Mental prayer is only a phrase—you cannot pray with your mind. You pray with your heart or with the depths of your being. The real origin of the expression "mental prayer" was to distinguish it from vocal prayer. If I were to recite the Breviary without moving my lips and without speaking aloud, I would be making mental prayer according to that definition. But mental prayer which would consist of just reasoning things out—that is not prayer. It may be thinking or concentrating, but it is not prayer. As for meditation, we have never really gone into it.

There is, of course, a traditional, simple kind of Christian meditation in the Western Church which has been basically valid from the beginning and is always valid. It is what the Benedictines call *lectio divina*, a special kind of meditative reading, and I think this probably works best and most simply for the majority of people. You take the Bible or some book that means a great deal to you, and you read quietly in such a way that when you get something to chew on you stop and chew. If you want to stop and look out the window, you stop and look out the window. There is nothing wrong with doing that. You may not feel that you are getting anywhere, but it is a good thing to do and very easy and simple. I think that at Gethsemani this is one thing all the monks enjoy to a great extent.

At Gethsemani we have the horarium set up. We have to do a certain amount of work every day—we still have to work and make our living—but there is a great deal of free time. We also have 2,000 acres of woods and anybody who wants to, when he has finished his work, can just grab a book and take off, go out and sit by a lake and read for two or three hours. Believe me, this is a blessing and a great luxury, and I hope that they appreciate it because really you have to be a millionaire to do something like that these days.

I would like now to talk a little bit about the theology of the Eastern Orthodox Church in which I am also interested and which I think is something that we might profitably explore in the present day. In the Western Church we are very much concerned with such ideas as justification—whether it is justification by faith, grace, nature, merit, all centering around the Cross as the solution to a legal problem. Man is in trouble with sin; how is he going to get out of this trouble? The Cross is the answer. And how are the merits of the Cross transmitted to us? Justification has been the traditional line taken by Western theology since the Middle Ages.

The Orthodox people say that this is insufficient. One of their

82

theologians in whom I am particularly interested is Vladimir Los-sky, who is now dead, but who was a teacher in Paris where there is an Orthodox seminary. Ever since the Revolution, people who escaped from Russia and some of whom were previously Marxist but who went back to the traditional Orthodox theology, have taught in Paris. There was in fact a great theological movement of the Orthodox before World War II—very fruitful, very rich—and Lossky is one of its leading theologians.

Lossky criticizes our Western theology for not having under-stood the role of the Holy Spirit and for not having a theology of the Holy Spirit. (I am not saying whether he is right or wrong.) To the West, he says, you really have no place for the Holy Spirit in your theology—he is just somebody extra, and, in order to fit him in every once in a while, you give him a little nod and invite him in and say he is really helping out by distributing the merits of Christ. But you really can't fit him in, you have no place for him. As a consequence, in Lossky's opinion, Confirmation is something that we don't know what to do with, an extra sacrament. It be-comes the equivalent of the Jewish Bar Mitzvah—an entrance into adolescence.

The Eastern Orthodox emphasize strongly, first of all, what they call the economy of God. (Economy is just a fancy word for house-keeping, from the Greek word for house.) How does God run his household? This is what is revealed in the Bible. It is not a question of explaining who God is, for the Bible does not really explain any-thing about the mystery of God in himself. The Bible just explains what God does with us, his promises to us; how, in fact, he runs his household. This economy, this plan of God is centered on the fact that man is the image of God, and that God comes down to earth and empties Himself to save man, and the restoration of man is the work of the Holy Spirit. So the reality of the Christian mystery is precisely the work of the Holy Spirit, and the most important reality of the present age, which is the eschatological age, the last age, is therefore that everything is in the hands of the Holy Spirit.

This is the age of the Holy Spirit—the Holy Spirit given as a fruit of the Resurrection, as a result of the Resurrection, and the Holy Spirit is here transforming us, overcoming death in us, and communicating to us the incorruptibility and the risen life of the new creation which is the risen Christ. The Holy Spirit, therefore, is at work in us, not just to remind us to look back to the Passion and remember where it all started, but to communicate to us the fruits of the Passion and of the Resurrection and to create in us the risen life or the victory over death. Consequently, what we get from this is an economy of the Holy Spirit in which the Holy Spirit is absolutely essential.

Lossky says that the trouble with the Western Church is that instead of our having a theology of the Holy Spirit, we have a sacramental system, and everything is tied up in this machinery, this process of sanctification by sacraments. The Orthodox have sacraments, and Lossky is not downgrading the sacraments but saying that we apparently fail to see where the Holy Spirit is operating. It isn't a process; it is the Holy Spirit. It isn't machinery; it is the action of the Holy Spirit. He says, "We risk the loss of personal liberty and we risk, after having been saved from the determinism of sin, falling into a kind of sacramental determinism (this may be too strong) where an organic process of salvation accomplished in the collectivity of the Church tends to suppress personal encounter with God." Western theology, he says, tends to be institutional, and even though there is a theology of the Mystical Body, it tends to be a collective theology rather than a theology of the Holy Spirit. This

84

is typically Orthodox. The central idea of Orthodoxy is what they call *sobornost*, which is community in the Spirit, and the great idea of Orthodox theology is this building of community in the Spirit where we are transformed in the living, risen Christ. In other words, what he is saying is that we are tempted, as Westerners, to be collectivists rather than personalists. We are afraid to act as persons, afraid to act under the individual and special inspiration of the Holy Spirit.

Of course, one must be a little careful about this. You have to know how to judge what is right, but we tend to be afraid to follow our consciences in a simple way. You may say, "There are a lot of people following their consciences and making an awful lot of noise about it." I think the reason they make so much noise about it is that they are insecure. If a person is securely following his own conscience, he doesn't have to challenge the whole world about it. If, in order to justify following my conscience, I have to break down the doors of the Synod or set fire to the White House, there is something the matter with my conscience and I am probably a pretty insecure person. According to the theology of the Holy Spirit, we have received the Holy Spirit, and if you enter into conflict with somebody you will resolve the situation in some way because you are following the Holy Spirit. If you think you are following the Holy Spirit and are hitting somebody over the head, then you have a pretty good indication that what you are following is not the Holy Spirit. The Holy Spirit is the Spirit of love, so you must respect the other person and love the other person and go along, insofar as you can, with him.

In Russian theology there is an almost exaggerated kenoticism or self-emptying. One of the great examples they give is of two Russian martyrs who actually allowed themselves to be murdered

85

by a third brother. They were princes and they were all legitimate heirs to a kingdom or an estate, and the third brother wanted it all, so they said, "O.K., if you want it, go ahead and kill us," and he killed them. This is typical of Russian exaggerated kenoticism, but it indicates a truth and reminds me of a story.

Two Desert Fathers had been living together as hermits for many years and had never gotten into a fight. One of them said to the other, "Why don't we do like everybody else in the world and get into a fight?" The other fellow said, "O.K., how to you do it?" He said, "Well, fights start over possessions, owning something exclusively so that the other fellow can't have it. Let's look around and get ourselves a possession and then have a fight over it." So he found a brick and said, "I will put this brick between us and I will say, 'This is my brick,' and you will immediately say, 'No, it is mine,' and then we will get into a fight." So the man gets the brick and puts it down between the two of them and says, "This is my brick." And the other says, "Well, brother, if it is your brick, take it."

Russian kenoticism, as I said, is exaggerated, but there is a real truth underlying it: if a person is led by the Holy Spirit he no longer has any kind of a self that he defends. He is not defending himself, he is going with the Holy Spirit.

We misunderstand personality completely if we think, "My personality is nothing but my little exclusive portion of human nature." Because it isn't. That is my individuality; when I die that individuality has either got to disappear immediately or has to go through purgatory and be gotten rid of there. Personality is not individuality. Individuality is exclusive; personality is not. Each one of us has an individuality which is exclusive, but that is not the whole story, and that is not the person that you are trying to fulfill. If you try to fulfill an exclusive individuality as if it were a person, you end up in complete self-contradiction, because what the person really is is an existence for others, and the pattern for that is the Trinity.

The divine persons don't have three pieces of the divine nature. They have one divine nature and each one exists unto the others, for the others. Perhaps you begin to see something of the sense of the refusal to assert one's own exclusive individuality in the presence of the other, of being completely open to the other. On the other hand, you cannot at the same time be completely absorbed in the other. There has to be a certain distance. How do you reconcile the fact that the person is not just an exclusive little fence around a section of nature and yet is different and unique? You have to combine uniqueness and complete openness and non-exclusiveness, and the only answer to that is the Holy Spirit. The Holy Spirit is the one who confers on the human person this particular character of being completely open and yet being nonetheless completely unique.

To me that is the key to the whole question of Christian personalism, and I think that it is the Orthodox who have the key, not the French existentialists and other such groups. It is a theology which can be found in Orthodox tradition and found in our tradition also, because it goes back to the Greek Fathers and to the Latin Fathers. Saint Basil says that the Spirit finds himself present in each one as if he were communicating to him alone and yet imparts to all a common grace.

If you can understand that and really absorb it, you can see the whole meaning of prayer and the whole meaning of Christian personalism. And if you see that, you understand there is really no opposition, as we still tend to think there is, between praying alone and being with people. Both are true, both are right, and you don't divide one against the other and say it is purely horizontal or it is purely vertical. It is both horizontal and vertical and you should follow what is right for you at a given time. When you are dealing with people, for as long as it works go on dealing with people; when you get tired of dealing with people, go pray alone. There comes a time when you just get tired of a particular prayer form unless you have a charism of never getting tired of it! All right, that is your charism, your thing. But most of us should simply follow the natural rhythm of the way we are constituted and follow the Holy Spirit. There is a time and place for everything.

One of the most beautiful books in the Bible is the Book of Ecclesiastes in which you have that wonderful chapter: "There is a time for weeping and a time for laughing . . ." (3:1-9). The Holy Spirit deals with us on the basis of these natural alterations, and what we have to avoid is saying this alone is the right way or that alone is the right way. We need to be able to move freely with the Spirit in prayer as each situation demands. That is the real secret of the life of prayer, and that is what the life of prayer is for.

Lossky points out the importance of Confirmation and how it gives you this freedom of operation. Confirmation is the sacrament of personal freedom and personal autonomy in the Spirit. He says that the sacrament of Baptism, the sacrament of unity in Christ, must be completed by the sacrament of Chrismation, the sacrament of diversity in the Spirit. And there you have what I think is a complete theology—a theology in which the gift of the Spirit grants us this complete liberty and freedom to be ourselves without infringing on others.

This is extremely important. It is awfully easy to be free while at the same time infringing on everybody else. And this so often happens. But it is a special gift of the Spirit to be free without violating the rights of others, and to fulfill love without violating love. I don't intend any lack of respect for Western theology, but it does seem to me that there is a great value in this Orthodox concept. It is important anyway, to the West as well as to the East, to remember that we all need the Holy Spirit, not as something extra, something remembered as an afterthought, but as an ever-present reality, an integral part of our lives.

The Holy Spirit is central and primary in our present stage of existence because it is he who is carrying on the work of forming the new creation and of transforming all in Christ and restoring all in Christ. Prayer must be seen in that context. What follows from that is, as far as prayer is concerned, that you can do what you like so long as it makes sense, and the one thing to avoid or not to do is to get hung up on any one thing and say, "This is the only thing, and everybody who doesn't do this is wrong." All the old ways are good and all the new ways are good. We can't do everything, so you pick the way that is good for you at the time that it is good for you.

❧

REPLY TO A QUESTION PRESUMABLY ABOUT CHANGES IN THE DIVINE OFFICE:

All I can say is what our communities are doing. They have an experimental Office in which they can juggle things around as much as they want. Apparently it is difficult for people today to concentrate on a long succession of psalms. So these communities have one psalm, a little silence, a long reading, silence, another psalm, silence, a long reading, another psalm, and a concluding oration. It is just a question of changing the balance so that it corresponds more to our present attention span. In prayer you must be awake and attentive and aware of what goes on, and it should never become automatic. We seem to have a better capacity to sit and listen to somebody reading than we have to recite psalms together.

Another of the things we do is for one person to read a psalm all by himself while the others listen. There is nothing revolutionary about this. This is exactly what the first monks did. The Office of the earliest desert monks consisted, to a great extent, of somebody standing up and reading a psalm while the others listened. Then there was a long mental prayer or meditation, then a spontaneous collect where the leader brought everything together in one short prayer. Then another one would read a psalm and the others would listen, and so on.

What I would also suggest is that those who are really involved in working on new forms of the Office will have an opportunity to visit places where they are experimenting and where they are doing it well. Some communities are writing some very good music of their own, and they also dance in the Office once in a while, on some special occasion. After Mass on the last day of a workshop at at a certain community, one of the nuns who is a very good dancer came out, in habit but barefoot, and danced right around the sanctuary and around the altar, and it was beautiful.

ANSWER TO ANOTHER QUESTION:

This whole question of the Blessed Sacrament seems to be a false argument. For some people the Blessed Sacrament is a great help, and they should pray before the Blessed Sacrament. It does not mean necessarily that this is the *only* way for everybody to pray, but for some people—for me—it is a help. I didn't realize how true this was until I moved into my hermitage and was not allowed to have the Blessed Sacrament. This went on for a couple of years, and I didn't even think about it really until somehow or other the issue came up again and I was given permission to have the Blessed Sacrament reserved at the hermitage. I found it was a great help. One of the things that was nicest about it—well, I would lie in bed and if I woke up, there was the tabernacle. This is a real, simple, naive sort of thing, but actually it made me feel quite different at night, just the sense of this Presence. There is nothing nicer than that. That is beautiful, I think, for hermits anyway.

But let's respect individual differences and let each one do what is best for him or her and not feel badly if nobody else is doing it. Suppose you have a community of a few people and you are the only one who wants to pray before the Blessed Sacrament. Well, go ahead and do it. Why not? That is your thing, and there should not be any problem about that. But we tend too much towards a collective mentality and we are too much hung up on the idea that everybody has got to be doing the same thing. If it is right, then you should all do it, and if you should not all do it, then what is the matter with it? Is it wrong? We are not used enough to the idea that several people can be right in different ways, and there can be different ways of being right.

Building Community on God's Love

Eberhard Arnold[1] wrote this at a time of great tension, when Germany was under Hitler's rule. It is really a fine Gospel statement of community against the background of false community being spread by the Nazis. It may also be seen against the background of the present mystique of community that you find with the Communists, which is rather attractive to many Catholics today because there is an idea that Marxism may have a solution and that revolution is really a Christian solution. As you know, there is quite a strong trend among progressive Catholics towards this concept of real community. Eberhard Arnold sees both sides of the picture and comes out with what I think is a completely Christian answer. But before we start considering our vocation and our life basically in this context, we have to stop and think what our Lord was doing, what did He come into the world for? What did He die on the cross for? What was His aim? Because that necessarily affects our aim, and it affects what we are doing.

The standard answer always used to be, "He came to die for sinners." That is to say, we are converted from sin, we don't have to go

---

1. One must assume that Thomas Merton started this conference with a reading from a work of the German Lutheran theologian, Eberhard Arnold—possibly from a book called *Living in Community*, published in this country by Plough Press, Rifton, New York.

to hell, we can go to heaven if we behave ourselves. And that is a really crude answer, because there is so much more in it than that. Our Lord came to overcome death by love, and this work of love was a work of obedience to the Father unto death—a total gift of Himself in order to overcome death. That is our job. We are fighting death, we are involved in a struggle between love and death, and this struggle takes place in us. Our Lord's victory over death, the victory of love over death on the cross, seeks to be manifested in a very concrete form on earth in the creation of community. The work of creating community in and by the grace of Christ is the place where this struggle goes on and where He manifests His victory over death.

Let's take a quick look at Saint Paul. There may be many better quotations on this point, but this is about us—we are chosen for this life, yet we are just ordinary people, people with our own limitations, as Saint Paul stresses in the famous passage of I *Cor.* 1:26-31: "Take yourselves for instance, brothers, at the time when you were called; how many of you were wise in the ordinary sense of the word, how many were influential people, or came from noble families?" (The old text was: "Consider your vocation"—consider this fact: who are we who are called to share in the work of Christ, the superhuman work of overcoming death?) "No, it was to shame the wise that God chose what is foolish by human reckoning; those whom the world thinks common and contemptible are the ones that God has chosen—those who are nothing at all to show up those who are everything. The human race has nothing to boast about to God, but you, God has made members of Christ Jesus and by God's doing he has become our wisdom, and our virtue, and our holiness, and our freedom. As scripture says, 'If anyone wants to boast, let him boast about the Lord.'"

So, here we are in this job of building community, which is what Christ died for, and whom does He pick to build community? He picks us, just ordinary people with ordinary weaknesses. Some of the people who have come to Gethsemani with the best minds don't have vocations; often the ones who do have vocations are the ones who are always going to struggle along with their weaknesses and the ordinary problems of life. We must take this for granted, that God has this design, this plan, and He chooses whom He will, and most of us are just ordinary people. We have to see ourselves in that light and in that context to understand what community means.

Eberhard Arnold, in treating of community, starts out by making quite clear something that I don't think is clear enough right now. The big thing today is community. People think in terms of community and also in terms of personal fulfillment, and these are good things. But at the same time, with this great ferment about community, there is a danger of—what would you say? Let me give you an example.

I noticed in the ecumenical field that something strange suddenly started to happen about five or six years ago, just about the time of the opening of the Council. Protestants who disagreed with others of their denomination would come to us, and we who disagreed with other Catholics would go to them. So you found Baptists and Catholics and Presbyterians and Episcopalians who were discontented with their own bunch huddling together in a new group. This is something that tends to happen. As we open up to more people outside the old community, we tend to form other communities. You find new grounds of sympathy; people with a new look and a whole new background, and you are stimulated by the first contacts and perhaps you become more involved with

95

them than with your own community. This happens and actually is normal.

The reason for it is probably because we are also in the midst of swinging away from an old situation in which community was rather abstract and what you really had was an organized institution instead of a real community. You had a lot of rules and everything was all set and people did the same thing at the same time and were in the same place at the same time and acted as a community, and probably there was a great deal of charity present in that way of life. But it was also quite possible in this perfect institution to hide an almost total absence of true community. It did cut down on big problems but in a way it created even bigger ones. The fact that everything was so much like a machine made it possible to go through all the motions without any real love, or, at least, without any deep personal love for the people you lived with.

At the point I am describing, say ten years ago, people suddenly realized that there was a paralysis in the institutional community, that it was static and even a little bit false and liable to breed all sorts of odd things. Instead of deep personal love, you had sentimental attachments. It was all part of that old picture where the life was so closed in and people tended to develop mushy attachments instead of real love. When things suddenly opened up and everyone was getting back into more normal contacts, there was a very strong reaction. People felt, "Here is a healthy community that we have with our friends and this is real." And it was more real than the old institutional community, but neither one is the real thing, neither one is the community that Christ came to build. As Eberhard Arnold says, there is more to it than just this personal fulfillment, which is good, and there is more to it than sociability, which is also good.

96

There is something deeper than that and what Arnold works on first, being a Protestant, is to point up something that we Catholics don't always see very clearly because our theology is more optimistic—the fact that there is basic optimism about natural community which tends to ignore the struggle of life and death in us. What he wants to stress—and I think the Protestant always stresses this too much—is the fact that community is not built by man, it is built by God. It is God's work and the basis of community is not just sociability but faith. This is what we really need to see very clearly, because it is very important. So then, turning to the idea of a community built on God—because that is really the center of Christianity—the Church is God's community, the Church is the work of Christ, and when I say this I don't mean just religious community. It is Christian community, the body of Christ, life in Christ.

At the other extreme you have the story I mentioned earlier about the two old hermits who had never quarreled, the idyllic community. It is a screwball story, an exaggeration, a typical Desert Fathers' story, but there are two points to it. Most important—the real theological content of the story—is that what really starts fighting is possessions. And people get into fights by preferring things to people. This is well developed in Christian theology, and therefore, for us, the importance of detachment from things, the importance of poverty, is that we are supposed to be free from things that we might prefer to people. You can extend that to any limits you like—wherever things have become more important than people, we are in trouble. That is the crux of the whole matter. Figure it out for yourself!

One of the Greek Fathers, Saint Maximus, has an interesting development of this which at one time I wrote up as a basic theology of peace and non-violence. He takes this point and works it up to show how the root of war is really in preferring possessions to human values and money to human beings, which is absolutely true. If you look at Vietnam you can really see the heart of the matter. It is investments and material interests that are at stake for the most part, although we certainly do want to protect freedom. That is our expressed desire, but in fact what is happening is that a great many people are being killed and a great deal of money is being made on it. That's how it actually ends up, which shows there is something wrong with it.

To get back to our proposition: what God wills is the construction of community in Christ, and our job as religious, one of our big responsibilities, is to build community in any way we can. But it must be a real community, in every possible way, remembering the prior, objective right of our own community in which we have vows, because that means that we are obligated first to the people we are living with. It is like marriage to some extent, viewed in terms of objective obligations.

But that is not our only obligation. Very often we used to think that the only people we had to love were our fellow religious. Perhaps we never saw anyone else to love. No, we do have to love others and we want to love others and the community extends beyond our own community. The pattern seems to me to be this: in your particular case people come here to find a group of people who love one another. They don't come here merely to see you as individuals; they come to see you as a community of love. If they are going to find grace and help, it isn't so much from each one of you as an individual, but from the grace that is present in a community of love.

However we look at it, as religious and as priests, we have this obligation to build community; it isn't just an obligation to one another but to all those who come to us. They need to find true community here, and that is the best thing we can give them.

Here is another quotation from Saint Paul's great epistle to the Ephesians, the one on the mystical body. It is really a tremendous one to meditate on in this connection. I am always quoting it to show how community and contemplation and understanding the mystery of Christ are all linked together.

> "Do not forget, then, that there was a time when you who were pagans physically, termed the Uncircumcised by those who speak of themselves as the Circumcision by reason of a physical operation; do not forget, I say, that you had no Christ and were excluded from membership of Israel, aliens with no part in the covenants with their Promise; you were immersed in this world without hope and without God. But now in Christ Jesus, you that used to be so far apart from us have been brought very close, by the blood of Christ. For he is the peace between us, and has made the two into one and broken down the barrier which used to keep them apart, actually destroying in his own person the hostility caused by the rules and decrees of the Law. This was to create one single New Man in himself out of the two of them and by restoring peace through the cross, to unite them both in a single Body and reconcile them with God. In his own person he killed the hostility. Later he came to bring the good news of peace, peace to you who were far away and peace to those who were near at hand. Through him both of us have in the one Spirit our way to come to the father.
>
> "So you are no longer aliens or foreign visitors; you are citizens like all the saints, and part of God's household. You are part of a building that has the apostles and prophets for its foundations, and Christ Jesus himself for its main cornerstone. As every structure is aligned on him, all grow into one holy temple in the Lord; and you too, in him, are being built into a house where God lives, in the Spirit." (*Eph.* 2:11–22)

Paul is speaking of the Greek and the Jew—that there is no longer any division. It is one of the difficult passages of Saint Paul.

99

There is so much packed into it, and here is the idea he is always stressing: that the law created division, but the New Testament has overcome division which was created by the law; there is no longer any Jew or any Greek. In this creation of community, therefore, community is based not on ethnic background, not on whether you are a Jew or go to the synagogue, but on the love of persons in Christ, personal relationships in Christ, and it isn't based on nationality or class. And this is where Christians fail so often today.

A politician can go around saying he stands for God, when what he really stands for is racism, and so racism becomes equated with Christianity. This is idolatry, it is turning things inside out. And it is the same with nationalism—people say we will equate our national outlook with Christianity and suddenly all these things which have absolutely nothing to do with Christianity become identified with Christianity. This is a serious problem because it is a great scandal to people who have trouble with faith today. They say, "If this man is really a Christian, how can I be a Christian?"

I do want to emphasize the fact that, in Himself, on the cross, Christ destroyed the hostility that was created by all these divisions. There again is what community means for us, destroying division by the cross. In other words, we must be bigger than divisions. There will still remain ethnic differences, but they no longer make any difference in Christ. I think that where the real trouble comes is that we have a tendency—it's a sort of American myth—to think that this is all very simple and natural. All you have to do is follow your natural good tendencies and it is all taken care of. It isn't. It isn't automatic, it has to be done by God. It is a work of God.

As Eberhard Arnold says, we really do experience in ourselves at the same time as the power of Christ, the power of the cross to create community. We find in ourselves everything that goes against community, and we have to be completely aware of this fact. We are and we are not communal people. It is taken for granted that we are all really sociable. But we are and we aren't. We are also weak and selfish, and there is in us this struggle between trust and mistrust, where we all believe and don't believe. We trust other people and we distrust other people. We are, in other words, full of ambivalence, and we must take this into account. Things are in reality so much more complicated. We assume that we are perfectly open and trusting and then suddenly we discover that we aren't. When we live together with people we have strong feelings of rebellion against them, we really rise up against them. This has to be understood. What we tend to do is to deny this, repress it; we don't like to face it. But we just have to face the fact that sometimes we get darned mad at people, we get worked up about it and we do our best not to show it, but there it is. You cannot possibly live religious life realistically unless you realize that this is going on all the time.

The reason we repress our feelings is that they cause anxiety. If I admit to myself that I feel mad and angry, then right away I think what will this lead to? We will be fighting like cats and dogs for months to come, if I show my real feelings. What are you to do? From a natural point of view, in a certain sense, you are right. Then where are you going to go for help? You go to God. In other words, instead of basing our confidence on our ability to repress these feelings and keep them out of sight, what we have to do is to take a whole new attitude and say, "All right, I have these feelings and I know they are there. I am sorry about them, but the grace of Christ can fix it, the grace of Christ in me and the grace of Christ in my brother and sister." It isn't just that I have the grace—the point is that the community has the grace. You have sufficient grace to

101

solve all your problems in the ordinary human way; that is to say, to deal with them, not to be without them. You have to work at it all the time, but you do have the solution. So rejoice; you have nothing to worry about, but you do have some work to do.

There is no doubt of the final result, but it isn't because of you. It is because of Christ. It will be fine, it will work out all right. All this is especially true today when with all our creativity we are also extremely destructive. Take the atom bomb. The discovery of atomic energy is one of the most fantastic creative break-throughs in the history of man, and it also resulted in one of the most fantastic destructive potentials of man. Then there are all the people crowded together in cities in huge numbers such as we have never had before. The cities could be the most magnificent civilization that ever happened, but they are also terribly destructive. This is our present condition.

Let's read a little bit of Eberhard Arnold and what he says about this problem: "Our common life is built from God as from the source of life, and is led ever anew to tragic struggles and ultimate victory. In a common life given in this way, there can be no seeking for idyllic human sociability or leisurely comfort. No kind of satisfaction of romantic desire or egotistical longing for personal happiness can be found here. On the contrary, this way of unconditional will to love of God's will for community, leads us straight into the reality of work and its fight for existence, into the reality of all the difficulties of human character. It is a way of deadly danger and of hardest suffering."

This may be a bit exaggerated ("deadly danger"); it isn't deadly danger but it's rough. "Yet just this is our deepest joy that we see clearly this tragedy of life, this tremendous tension between life and death, this situation between heaven and hell, and in spite of it all believe in the overwhelming power of Light, in love's power to overcome and in the triumph of truth because we believe in God." I think that is a pretty inspiring statement.

We must believe in community and believe that in God all this is possible. He goes on, "This faith is not a theory . . . it is a receiving of God himself. It is the being overwhelmed by God. Thus it is the strength to go the way. It is the actual possibility of trusting again and again where, looked at humanly, that which has been built by trust has been destroyed." This whole question of believing in God, of trusting in one another and yet knowing that trust can fall and can be rebuilt, all this is part of our life.

Then Arnold makes a statement which I think is extreme. He says, "It faces up to the fact that men, as their nature is now consti- tuted, are incapable of community." (That is going too far; it is Lutheran pessimism. Man is fallen and can't achieve community at all. That is not true. Saint Thomas wouldn't agree with it, but a statement like that nevertheless has some value because, even though it is exaggerated, it points to the fact that we really need God, and it is the need of grace that Arnold is bringing out.)

"The changing moods of the disposition, the possessive impulses . . . all these place a humanly insurmountable human barrier in the way of actual and real community building, and faith does not succumb to the delusion that these factual realities are decisive."

That is the great point. Suppose all these things are there, and supposing it is tough, the thing that faith does is to make a final judgment. Apply this to a marriage problem. Supposing a man discovers his wife has been unfaithful to him. This is one of the tragic kinds of violation of trust in life. It destroys people. So, this husband finds out. If he is the kind of person who says, "This is the end," then you have a certain type of human situation and human solution. But for faith this would not be decisive. It isn't necessarily the only answer.

What lies behind this statement of Arnold's is that in Nazism, in Hitlerism, there was a very different kind of pessimism, a really profound, almost diabolic pessimism. For Hitler such decisions are really superficial. If a man is a Jew, this is decisive. If he has any Jewish blood in him at all, back to the camps.

I did a study of the Nazi mind at one time, on Auschwitz, and this seemed to me at the heart of the problem—this absolute un-forgivingness. From the moment the slight flaw is discovered, fin-ished! That's the end. He is condemned. It is just the opposite with Christ. Even the greatest fault is forgivable, everything is forgiv-able. For Hitler and for anyone with that type of mentality, noth-ing is forgivable. And for us everything is forgivable.

"Here it becomes very clear that it is out of the question for real community to come into being, for the actual life in common to be built up where there is no faith in the ultimate power of God's love. All human efforts to trust again and again in the goodness that is actually in man, in spite of all adversities, are bound to break in pieces against the reality of evil." Again, this is too strong, but the conclusion is true: "Only faith in the ultimate mystery of good in God is able to build community."

The ultimate thing is that we build community not on our love but on God's love, because we really do not have that much love ourselves, and that is the real challenge of the religious life. It puts us in a position where sometimes natural community is very diffi-cult. People are sent here and there, and often very incompatible people are thrown together. Groups of people who would never have chosen to be together in an ordinary human way find them-selves living together. O.K. This is a test of faith. This puts God's love to the test and it is meant to. It is what Saint Paul means. It isn't just a question of whether you are building community with people that you naturally like, it is also a question of building community with people that God has brought together.

Here it is not much of a problem, but in Gethsemani there is such a big variety of people that it is quite evident. At one time we used to have all sorts of nationalities and there was quite a struggle. In World War II the Abbot didn't dare give news out because there were a lot of Germans in the community. I remember one of them: he was German-American. When the war broke out he entered the priesthood. "I am not going to fight against Germany, I am going to be a monk." He became a very good monk, but his basic idea was that Germany was all right and he was not going to get into war with his own country. It is easy to get into fights over things like that.

What is tested in the community's choice is faith. It is not so much a question of who's right, but do we believe? I think that is the real issue. Of course there are rights, but you put them all together and work them out on the basis and in the context of faith. Faith is first, and who is right is God. God is the one who is right; no one of us knows precisely what God wants. What we have to do is believe in the power of His love. This power is given to us in proportion as we work together to find out what the score is, and then, if we do get together and decide on something even if it is mistaken, still if it is in good faith, the power of God's love will be in it. We are going to make mistakes, but it really doesn't matter that much.

Community, Politics, and Contemplation

I want to talk a little bit more about community because in the Church today you have a very strong and active movement that you run into everywhere, in which a whole lot of people—a minority but a very influential minority of whom I know many—say that there is only one real community in existence today and that is the community which is concerned with the problems of underprivileged people, that the only practical way of handling this is revolution and that, therefore, Christianity equals revolution.

People talk in this way and there is going to be trouble because they don't really know what they are talking about. They are all good, middle-class people who have become priests and nuns, and all of a sudden they are talking about revolution.

There is a temptation now of looking for community when you are concerned over political things. After all, you can't avoid it really, you have to be concerned about the world and about politics in some way. But on the other hand, just aligning yourself with somebody else's movement is not necessarily the answer. A good Quaker friend of mine, who was a friend of Martin Luther King, was very much involved in civil rights in the South in an absolutely disinterested and dedicated way. She and her husband became involved in a demonstration in Washington. They had absolutely the highest motives but they joined up with some activists who didn't seem to have the highest motives at all, and they found themselves forced by these people into a weird situation in which they were all arrested. They had been forced to break a law they never intended to break and didn't want to break so that they could be used and the activists could say, "So-and-so was arrested on our side."

In other words, when you start dealing with people of this sort you are not dealing with community in any Christian sense, you are dealing with a bunch of operators and they have their reasons, but they are in power politics and this is dangerous. You are probably not going to run into much of all this up here in Alaska, but people in your position in the lower forty-eight states are going to meet Catholic activists, perhaps coming for a retreat or a conference, and they are going to be fermenting with these ideas and we really have to know what the score is.

I personally think that we should be in between; we shouldn't be on the conservative side and we shouldn't be on the radical side —we should be Christians. We should understand the principles that are involved and realize that we can't get involved in anything where there is not true Christian fellowship. You do have a great deal of good will in these movements and you do have a kernel of desire for community, but power takes priority. The power play is the important thing and you come up against not love but love-less means. Most activists do not go in for naked violence yet, but they will. In other words, there are ways and means to force people to go in a certain direction. That is okay, that is politics, you might say. If you are a politician you need to know about it and deal with it, but we have to stay out of it.

Writing in the thirties in Germany, Eberhard Arnold was caught between the Nazis and the Communists. The Nazis were the absolutely brutal type of community which is simply racism—just crude emotion, lining everybody up and marching them off. This is a sort of massive, fanatical community which I am afraid you are going to get more of in this country. I don't think the whole country will ever be behind it, but there are going to be some people in this country of this type, and Catholics are going to be caught between that and the radical extreme. There will be people who are scared and just want to protect their property; and people at the other end will be mixed up in this so-called revolutionary action.

Arnold saw all this and what he concluded is the position that I pretty well agree with, too—it is the Spirit who is above both these positions and we have to keep above them, too. We have to be where love is and it is really the harder position, but it is also the creative position, and the constructive position. It is the kind of position taken by Gandhi.

It is not at all just an idealistic position because Gandhi took it. I edited and wrote a preface for a little book of quotations from Gandhi on non-violence, and perhaps it is good to remember it because it all tends to get lost now. Non-violence has become all fouled-up and is turning into a sort of semi-violence. But the basic thing Gandhi said, and it has proved absolutely right, is that you can't have any real non-violence unless you have faith in God. If it isn't built on God, it isn't going to work, it isn't going to be real. Gandhi said this and Martin Luther King picked it up and carried it on. So there you have the spiritual approach and it was based on asceticism. Gandhi primarily used to fast and use spiritual means. So what we have to do is try to distinguish between this temptation to seek community in all sorts of power movements, as so many are doing, and to maintain our position in a Christian community —a community built by God.

It is of just this situation that Arnold says, "It follows that we must live in community. Because there is all this yearning for community in these other forms that we have to form our Christian community. All revolutions, all voluntary associations of idealists and life-reformers have given proof both of their longing for community and their incapacity for community." The Communists talk up community in the greatest possible way. If anybody disagrees with them, WHAM . . . Czechoslovakia starts building its own community and in they come with their tanks, which is a tragedy.

What does Arnold mean by "associations of idealists and life-reformers?" There is a footnote about vegetarians going off in groups and also a reference to people rather like the hippies. The hippies are in many ways real good kids. They manifest this desire for community and yet a kind of incapacity for it, so they sort of float around in groups.

I didn't tell you about this hippie down at Christ in the Desert, a really lovely guy. He is not just an ordinary hippie, I think he is deeper. He met me at the plane when I went there and he had this really long hair, with a red leather thong like an Indian to keep it from falling in his eyes while he was driving. A very nice guy. He had this beat-up old Volkswagen station wagon with a stove in the back and a bed where he lived. He was towing a plaster mixer and I asked him, "What have you got that for?" He said, "I figured I was going to do something for the monks and I am going to work for them for a year and make them bricks for their guest house." He just decided to do that. He is not necessarily a Christian and he is not a Catholic, but he is living at the monastery and he wants to help the monks out. He wants a place to think, so he's got his Volkswagen back in the canyon under a tree, and he makes these bricks. He is just absolutely the nicest guy you ever saw. We rode all the way up to Albuquerque, up to the monastery, and all he wanted to talk about was meditation. How do you meditate? What do you do and what do the Hindus do? What do the Buddhists do? He was interested in prayer and he told me all about his life, how he had been in the Army and finally realized that it wasn't making any sense. Now he wanted to try to find out what it was all about so he went to live in a canyon in his Volkswagen.

You probably don't get that many hippies up here, but you may run into some sometime because they would be naturals to gravitate towards monasteries, just because they want community.

At The Redwoods there are some wonderful hippies. As soon as they moved into the area and found out that there was a monastery, they all came over and brought food. In fact, they have had a couple of parties there, in the garage, with everyone playing guitars and singing and the hippies each one doing his own thing, playing what he could play, and they all enjoyed it. This is an example of the desire for community which is all around.

Eberhard Arnold says, "All these attempts drive us to the recognition again and again that faith in the good, that the will to community which lies hidden as a mystery in all revolutions—because that is what is there—can only be made vital through one thing, through that which brings to light the clear example of deed and the word of truth, both deed and word as one in God, and of course as one in Christ." Our Lord on the cross is both word and act of God, giving the foundation. "And we have only one weapon to fight the conditions today and this weapon of the Spirit is the constructive work in the fellowship of love." This is the real basis of community, he says.

Then he takes up the idea that we can't be sentimental about community. It really means working together: "We know no sentimental love, no love without work. Just as little do we know a devotion in practical work which does not daily prove and give expression to the heart-to-heart relationship coming forth from the Spirit among those engaged to work together. The love of work, the work of love is a matter of the Spirit." He writes really well on community life; it is realistic and basic and the presence of the Spirit is proved by working together in love for a common end.

This, of course, ties in with the great aim of the Church today which the Council brought out so strongly in *Gaudium et Spes*, and the idea of Teilhard de Chardin—building the new world, collaborating towards the fullness of the maturity, the adulthood of man.

Arnold says this: "We acknowledge Jesus and early Christianity because they devoted themselves to man's outward life as much as to man's inner need. They never despised the body and the earth, but nevertheless were concerned with the soul and the spirit. When Jesus was asked about the future state of justice, He answered by pointing to His deeds—sick bodies were healed, men were raised from the grave, diabolic powers were delivered from tormented bodies, the message of joy was brought to the poorest people. The message means the invisible kingdom is at hand as the cause of the future, it is being realized now. God becomes flesh and ultimately and finally the earth will be won completely for God."

We are winning the earth completely for God by experiencing the life of love and working together with his power to transform the world. This is a really deep Christian concept which underlies everything that is going on in our life, and that is what contemplation is. Contemplation is the realization of God in our life, not just realization of an idea or something partial, but a realization of the whole thing—the realization that we belong totally to him and he has given himself totally to us. It has all happened and it is going on now.

You have to realize also that you don't really see this. It happens and you see it and you don't. You get glimpses of it, you believe it, your life is based on it, and sometimes it seems to be in complete contradiction or impossible, and yet it is there. It is the place we are always coming back to. What did Saint Paul say? "That will explain why I, having once heard about your faith in the Lord Jesus and the love that you showed toward all the saints, have never failed to remember you in my prayers and to thank God for you. May the God of our Lord Jesus Christ, the father of glory..." [here is what contemplation is] "give you a spirit of wisdom and perception of what is revealed to bring you to full knowledge of Him. May he enlighten the eyes of your mind so that you can see what hope His call holds for you." It is all tied up with hope, and hope is what you don't see. It is a hope which is present but in invisibility. Somehow you know it and you don't know it. "What rich glories He has promised the saints will inherit. How infinitely great is the power He has exercised for us believers. This you can tell from the strength of His power at work in Christ when He used it to raise Him from the dead and make Him sit at the right hand in heaven, far above every sovereignty, authority, power or domination."

This is very important. When you get into Saint Paul, every once in a while you get a lot of power, authority, and domination, and we tend to slide right through that. But it is very important as we will see when we go on to discuss prayer, because prayer is our real freedom. It is the liberation from the alienation that I have been talking about.

It is in prayer that we are truly and fully ourselves and we are not under any other power, authority, or domination. We have to see what that means. "He has put all things under His feet and made Him as the ruler of everything, the head of the Church which is His body, the fullness of Him who fills the whole creation." You have to spend your whole life going over and over again through a passage like this. It is the only way you can ever get anywhere with it. You don't just read it a few times and then read it with a commentary. You keep coming back to it, and maybe after fifty years of chewing on it you begin to see what it really means.

Prayer, Tradition, and Experience

It is always hard to talk about prayer because everybody prays in private, and everybody is different, and we have to learn to respect our differences and to understand that each one of us is going to have an individual approach. It really would not be right if everybody was exactly on the same level.

When you talk about prayer, you never know whether it makes sense to anybody else or not. You talk about what you think and you don't know if it is getting through at all. Prayer is not logical or reasonable because our relationship with God is not reasonable. There is nothing reasonable about the cross; it is completely unreasonable; it is illogical. What could be more illogical than for God to come down to earth and die on the cross? It is the most illogical thing that ever happened, but it happened because He did it, because He wanted to do it and because He loved us. There is no logic in love. Love is far beyond logic.

What we need is a theology that supports prayer, that goes with prayer and gives it structure because otherwise, if you have nothing but prayer and no theology, it is like having water and no pail to put it in. Prayer doesn't escape you, but if you do have a theology that can contain it, put outer limits around it, then you know where you are. You can stay with it, but it is the water, not the bucket, that counts. If you pay too much attention to the bucket, you forget about the water and you get into difficulties again. The bucket is useful but what you want is the water. That is the kind of theology you need and, of course, the Bible has it. Biblical theology gives you a container for prayer.

Nowadays you hear of priests telling people to stop praying. Are they suddenly crazy? What do they mean by this? To understand it you have to understand the background and see it in its right context. Part of the context is the God-is-dead idea. What do they mean by that? And the other part of the context is that everything is purely horizontal. What do they mean by that? If you should run into a retreat master who says, "I don't pray; why should you pray?" probably the best thing to do is not to be shocked but simply to try to see what he means. Perhaps it isn't as bad as it sounds!

To some extent this attitude does tie in with the people who say Christianity equals revolution. They tend to be the people who say, "I don't pray." They are really saying that their revolutionary action is their prayer, and you can respect their idealism. But in a certain sense it is a sad situation because the problem is that they throw everything into their actions, put all their eggs into one basket, and say, "What I do is *it*—it is my prayer, it is my love, it is my Christianity, it is my faith." You can get a situation where action becomes everything and where it is possible to find yourself associating with people who are operating in this sphere without any idealism at all, and you can get taken over without realizing what is happening.

Deeper than this is the problem of a wrong attitude toward God and toward prayer which is purely rationalistic. Somebody has said that the God of the prayer-manuals can love no one but himself. It is this God who is nothing but a mathematical first cause, running a big machine of which He presses the button to get glory for Himself out of it. This is terrible theology, but it is really not too wild a caricature of the manuals. If you try to fit prayer into that kind of structure you get something inhuman, and it is part of our problem because it is hard to get away from a structure that you studied devotedly. What did we all do when we were taking our theology? It went in one ear and out the other and we used it for examinations, but it was still there and some priests remain dominated by this purely mechanical formula. God is a great big machine, an impersonal, loveless kind of thing. This view of God makes, for instance, the problem of evil insoluble because you can't get away from the fact that if He operates in this way He is causing evil, or if He is not actually causing it He is permitting it, and you get into this vicious circle—"How does God allow people to sin?" These are not real problems; they become problems only when you have a rationalistic concept of God. Our prayer tends to fall into this pattern and it becomes falsified.

Any theology in which we pretend to justify God by reason is bound to be bad theology. You cannot do it. It is the theology of Job's friends. The Book of Job tells us a great deal about prayer. It says that here is a man who undergoes great evil and here are four people who come along and explain the evil logically and they tell Job why he is wrong and why he has to suffer. We talk about the patience of Job, but Job is not patient at all. In fact, he is mad at God and he is arguing with God and he is protesting against God and saying you are not right, you are wrong, you shouldn't be doing this to me. And what happens at the end of it is that God comes along and says Job is right.

This is real theology, because it is not logical. And the real theo-logical message of this is not that God hits people over the head to show that He is there but that our relations with God are person-to-person relationships, and that we don't deal with God according to some system. You don't look up in a book, asking yourself, "How do I talk to God about this?" Something evil has happened in your life. So you look in the book, and the book says, "God permits evil for your good," and you say, "Oh well, all right." There is nothing wrong with this, but the Bible says that if you really talk with God and say what is in your heart you are doing right. You speak to God as a child to a father and you go to Him and tell Him what you want Him to know and then He tells you what He wants you to know, and this puts it on a completely person-to-person basis. You don't get to God through a system. You speak from your heart. That is the basic idea, and that is what the Book of Job is saying. That is what prayer is and that is what we have to do. God is jealous of us precisely and not for His glory but for our freedom. He wants us to have this freedom and spontaneity and the reality of this personal love for Him.

You realize that prayer takes us beyond the law. When you are praying you are, in a certain sense, an outlaw. There is no law between the heart and God. The law is outside our intimate relationship with God and if you bring a law into the intimate relationships of your heart with God, you mess things up. Between the soul and God there are no laws. But that is not a natural situation; it is the result of the redemption, the result of Christ. In other words, if there are no laws, then there is no law of prayer, there are no systems. Systems are fine up to a point, but all they are for is to help you get to the point where there is no more system, where you deal with God absolutely in your freedom and His freedom. The difficulty, of course, is that we don't have that much freedom, and so we don't know what to do.

Saint Paul says it in other terms: "For the just man there is no law," i.e., for the person who is dealing with God honestly and in sincerity there is no law, at least in his dealing with God. That is why prayer is hard. It is much easier if there is a law. Actually you have to start with a law, a system, but after a while the only rule that there is in prayer is that you never say anything that you don't mean. If you don't mean anything, don't say anything. Don't speak when you don't mean it. But you seek a deeper level to just *be* with God, just to listen to God, or however you want to put it. It is too close for words.

Let's consider what kind of formation monks received in the early days. They didn't have a theological course. Where did they get their formation instruction? One of the things you should beware of, first of all, is the idea that the religious, the contemplative does not need any formation or education. We know this is wrong, but it has been very strongly emphasized in the past and we have all suffered from it: don't read too much; don't learn too much; don't let them get their hands on too much theology—it is bad for them. Philosophy, too, is bad for them, and what they don't know won't hurt them.

But what kind of formation *did* the earliest monks receive? First of all, the basic formation that every Christian gets is not just catechism. It is kerygma, it is the word of God announced. Kerygma is a very special thing. First, for kerygma to take place there has to be a community and a sense of community. They are called together to hear the word of God proclaimed, and a proclamation is not the same as instruction. This idea of kerygmatic theology was worked out in the fifties to a great extent, and it is a very important idea because it involved the hearer as well as the speaker. It is the living word proclaimed in a community and received by that community with a consciousness that it is receiving the word of God and that this is making present the thing that the word is about. You can see, in that particular process, that the action is in the *word*, not in the person announcing it. He may not be terribly competent, but all he has to do is to get the message out. When you are reading an epistle, for instance, you are announcing the word of God, and this presupposes a liturgical community because that is where the call to hear the word of God takes place. You have responded to the summons. You are the ecclesia, you are the ones called together, the Church, even here in your little chapel.

Once you have been called together for this act of the Church, it is a very special situation. The word has more solemnity and power. God Himself is active when the word is proclaimed there. Even if you are only having a Bible vigil and not a mass, the proclamation of the message of salvation makes present the mystery of the death and resurrection of Christ. Even though it is not sacramentally, not eucharistically, still in the word the mystery is made present.

The real education of the Christian community is something that God Himself gets into. God Himself teaches us. And what the human teacher has to do is to get in there just enough to be a channel and to let God work through him. I think it helps a great deal if he is fully conscious of this kerygmatic aspect of it, rather than emphasizing the information aspects. Information is all right, but there has to be much more to it than that.

In the early monastic tradition you have the story also of Saint Francis—kerygma leading to monastic vocation. Both Saint Anthony and Saint Francis received their vocation when hearing the word of God announced in the Church. Anthony walked in and heard the Gospel read: "Leave all things and come follow me." And so he headed for the desert. Saint Francis heard the Gospel that says, "Don't take any money in your purse, don't wear shoes. . . ." So off he went to the wandering life of poverty. In the proclamation of the word of God, you are already getting a certain amount of formation and education provided you are aware that it is going on.

It is also clear from some of the early monastic documents that they didn't get their entire formation in the liturgy. Actual instruction was given. One of the earliest monastic documents on this is a report from the Egyptian Desert in Cassian. John Cassian went to Egypt and then came back and brought with him reports of what was going on in Egypt in order to start monasticism in France. He is essentially a Western monk but with an Eastern background. One of the most interesting things in this report is that he gives us a summary of a talk by one of the old Desert Fathers when he is receiving a novice and giving him the habit. This is a solemn moment, a liturgical ceremony, and in his talk he gives a brief theology of the monastic life, which summarizes the whole thing. The heart of the whole talk is the cross.

What we need to get is essentially a theology of the monastic life that relates it to the cross and resurrection. The whole point is that the renunciation of the monk and of the religious is a participation in the cross of Christ. That is where it gets its meaning, and we have to keep that central in order to make sense out of it. Any monastic education you get should refer to this somewhere, so that it is always leading you back to it rather than going off in all directions about little points of theology.

I have studied some of our own Indians' spiritual training. In almost any tribe the young Indian had to go through a kind of novitiate. He was sent off into the mountains, into some rugged place perhaps on top of a cliff, to fast and pray. He was given instructions beforehand on what to do and he would mark out an area with the points of the compass, which made it into a cross-shaped place, and he had to stay within that area. While he was there fasting and praying he was supposed to have a vision (that was the object of his being there), and this vision would be of his own spirit-person. It was really a discovery of one's own deepest self. When the boy returned to the tribe he would obey this spirit-person in important matters such as hunting and fighting and be guided by it. Obviously he was talking to a spirit, but there was something in himself that had been released by this period of fasting and praying alone. He had access to a deeper level of his own being, a sort of sixth sense.

This is really interesting for us because we don't have anything like this any more. We used to have in monastic life a sort of guru-disciple relationship, something like the idea of a spiritual father in the Desert tradition and in the Russian tradition, someone who knows intuitively how to bring out what is deepest in a person and, believe me, that is what we really need. But it is very hard. It is a charism. You have to have someone special who can do it, but really that is what we need—something where we don't get a lot of information but a release of all that is deepest in us that we would like to have access to. We know it is there and yet we can't get to it.

That is really why I want to go to Asia. I want to find out how Asian Buddhists are trained because they have a long tradition. The whole purpose of their education is to get down into the depths of a person. A lot of it is secret, and in order to learn it I may have to go through the course. But in the Desert tradition, as we know it, the way a person was formed was by picking somebody and going to him personally because he felt this was the one to guide him. He would live with him in the same cell, and to begin with all he would do was to do the same thing this old monk did. When the monk prayed, the novice would pray and watch, too, how he prayed and listen to what he said and do the same things. And when he ate, the novice ate, and when he worked, the novice worked. Then the old fellow watched him and told him when he was doing wrong and said, "Do this" and "Do that." The most difficult part of it was that the novice had to manifest all his thoughts, and the old monk said, "That is O.K.," or "That is a bad one," or "Watch out for this one." So the novice was completely guided in all his actions and thoughts by this man. Then, if the old man was really charismatic, he would bring out in the novice the deepest power of prayer. There was a theological slant to this in the Christian tradition because they traced the old man back to the apostles, and there was a sort of apostolic succession there, and what the disciple was really getting into was, in a sense, being formed to experience Christ as the apostles had experienced Him.

Now that is really the heart of contemplative life. We are an awfully long way from the apostles, but still what a community is for us is a little group of disciples who know the Lord though they don't know Him according to the flesh as Saint Paul says. That is, we don't know the historical Christ, yet we know the spiritual Christ because He is present in our gathering as He was present with the apostles, and the model for that, of course, is the gatherings of the apostles after the Resurrection when the Lord was present with them.

So in monastic tradition as well as in Church tradition in general, what you are really supposed to be educated for is to experience Christ present in the community, to live in a community life in which Christ is present as He was with his disciples. That is what tradition means for us—handing on that experience.

But the whole idea of tradition has been fouled up in monasticism. Tradition has come to mean holding your hands like this because that is what they did in the motherhouse, and following these little customs, all of which are really the outer husks of the whole thing. It was reduced to that because way back somewhere somebody once thought if you did all these things it created the right atmosphere. But after six or seven hundred years this was no longer necessarily true, and we needed to throw it out.

Two priests were asking me today, "What about the rule and all that sort of thing?" And they are going to ask you about your rule. I told them you can't base an education purely and simply on the rule because a lot of the things in the rule have become irrelevant, a lot of them accidental. I don't know what your rule says, but some of the things in our rule are now completely irrelevant. They are good and fine, but people who come in and follow the rule can't relate it to anything that is really important in their own life, even though they will do it and be very good about doing it.

Take our former kind of silence. For a lot of people, the kind of old Trappist silence was really artificial. You never spoke except to your superiors. You made signs, and the way we made signs you could say anything. It was a little more work, but you could say anything you wanted, and you just went through the routine of learning a new language. For a lot of people this was a kind of sham. So what we have done now is that everybody can talk outside the night silence. The idea is to talk as much as is necessary and then quit. And they are doing that pretty well, I think. There are probably a few who talk everywhere and anywhere about anything, but it is more real that way because you are making a choice. Previously, you could make signs any time and say anything, which does not transmit any kind of experience of Christ's presence in the community. It just transmits the knowledge of a new sign language.

Just before the change came, the sign thing was really very funny with us. They were making all kinds of signs that were really sort of pun signs. There is a sign for cat which is like the whiskers of a cat. They made that sign habitually—and we never had any cats—but they made it for a caterpillar tractor. That is just one example, but we had hundreds of signs like this that represented sounds. There was a Brother Egbert, and they made the signs for egg and bird. Brother Hubert was U-bird. This was going on all over the place and people got all wound up learning this. It was nutty, and it got so nutty that people just couldn't take any more. In the novitiate you had to teach signs. That is the result of eight hundred years of nonsense. When it gets that way, you just have to quit. There is much in the old rule that is along those lines, and you can't base a monastic education on it.

In India, too, there is a lot of this stuff, a mish-mash, but they have preserved much more of the depth. If you go to Asia, a lot of people say you have to break through a lot of superficial stuff in order to get to the real thing, and it isn't easy. I was talking to the Indonesian ambassador in Washington. He is a deeply mystical person. He said, "If you go to my country, you have to plunge through layer after layer of ruins in order to get to the real thing, but when you get all the way down, there is the real thing." There is this real core, but you have to find the right people—they are all sort of hidden, and nobody ever gets to them really. You have to know who they are, and you have to get to them and live with them for a bit. The Tibetans are from a small country, not confused by contact with others and very highly trained, so I still think they have their original idea pretty clear, but that is going to be hard to get to.

I think it would be very valuable for you to know something about these Asian traditions. The reason my Abbot has allowed me to go over there is so that I can give people a rundown on what these Asian traditions are about that would be useful because they do have techniques of meditation that work. They are not theological, but it is good psychology. The Buddhist idea is strictly psychological purification. It is deliberately confined to psychology, there is no theology in it whatever, and Buddha absolutely refused to give any kind of theological message. He said, "I am just a man." They said, "Will you write us a rule and found us an order?" And he said, "No, no rule. If anybody wants a rule, let him write his own rule. I am not going to give you any rule." He told them just before he died, "You have to stand on your own feet, and you have to do the job for yourself. I am not going to give you any rule. I have given you the principles to follow, the basic principles of life you need to know. I have given you these, and you just go."

They all wrote rules a mile long, but still the basic idea is that you live this simple, fundamental, philosophical thing of "Don't get hung-up on yourself." The idea that ourself is really what we experience as ourself is illusory and to get hung-up on it is to get in trouble every time, so what you are going to have to try to do is to get unstuck from this illusion of self in order to get to your *real* self, which is not you but is really one with everybody else. . . . Pantheism, etc. Maybe the philosophy is bad, but actually it works to some extent.

Monastic education is education for experience. There is no reason for contemplative monasteries to exist if you are not able, in a

contemplative monastery, to develop a different kind of consciousness from that experienced outside. Not that the outside is bad,
but I mean you specialize in a certain kind of awareness of the
mystery of Christ. If there is no special advantage in our kind of
life, if you don't get any special fruit from it, there is no point to it
really. The fact that we just say prayers is not a sufficient justification. I think we have to be deeper people in a certain way. Not just
deeper in the sense that we are much wiser than everybody else,
but there has to be a deeper experience of life. Our education
should lead to that deeper experience.

Prayer and Conscience

I am not even going to attempt to talk about *how* to pray, which assumes that everybody is pretty much the same. Instead, let's look at and try to understand our idea of who we are—our identity. Prayer and identity go together. Who is it that prays? What is our concept of ourselves or our non-concept of ourselves praying? Who do we feel ourselves to be when we pray?

Everybody assumes that we know where prayer comes from, but we don't at all. This whole idea of the self is most mysterious. It doesn't enter into our heads to question it because we live with it, but it is still a most mysterious thing. So I am going to talk about conscience as a focal point of where prayer happens.

Conscience has a great deal to do with prayer, but conscience used in a much wider sense than usual. Normally we think of the moral conscience which decides between right and wrong, which is really a figment of the imagination to begin with. Stop and think about it. It is very hard to put your finger on it. Where is this conscience? What is it? We know how it acts. The real concept of conscience is something quite mysterious and also quite complex and on different levels. I said previously that you pray with your heart, you pray with your whole life. This is conscience when it gets close to the Biblical concept of heart. In the psalms, when you talk about the heart you are talking about a very deep kind of conscience, not the conscience that decides I should do this and not do that; it is something much more fundamental.

Our conscience is very close to our identity. I am what my decisions are, in a way. It is by the activity of my conscience that I create my identity and make my life what it is. In the deepest possible sense, conscience for some of the Rhineland mystics, for instance, is the place you experience union with God. Eckhart is always talking about the spark at the center of the soul. What is it? We know there is something to it. It is a metaphorical expression, but it obviously does refer to something.

There are different levels of conscience. You have conscience in the sense of a psychological conscience which is consciousness—it doesn't decide anything, it is a kind of general awareness—you are awake, you are present. Conscience and presence are related notions. Conscience, consciousness makes me present to myself. Conscience has a great deal to do with the presence of God. Usually we restrict the term to moral conscience, and that is restricting it too much. The deepest level of conscience is beyond both consciousness and moral conscience; it is beyond thinking and self-awareness and decision. It is the conscience of God in us, it is where the Holy Spirit operates.

Conscience is not just a psychological faculty. As you go through this lineup from consciousness through moral conscience to what you would call a kind of spiritual conscience, you find that in the depths of your deepest conscience there is something more than just you, and it is something theological. In other words, the deepest sense of conscience is conscience with grace, not just me, but the Holy Spirit and me.

That is what prayer is all about. Prayer is not really just a way of addressing God out there somewhere. Prayer is opening up this deepest conscience and consciousness, a mystical conscience and a mystical consciousness, in which God and I work together. It is not merely a faculty of my psychological being. The problem is that we do not have a theological idea of man, and even today—perhaps especially today—much of the new thinking about man and about prayer is confused and confusing because it starts from a totally different concept of conscience and consciousness.

The Christian idea of man starts with God and works down. It should start with the Biblical idea of man from the beginning of Genesis and say that God created man in his own image. We used to say that you cannot know man without knowing something about God. But the modern non-Christian, non-religious approach on which we Christians tend to build starts from man and then either goes nowhere or goes to God, from the bottom up. This causes problems for us in the contemplative life because what you get then is really a non-religious and basically non-Christian idea of man based on a psychology and a sociology in which God is irrelevant. What you end up with is a sort of secular cake with a Christian icing.

To me this creates all kinds of problems. It is actually the concept of man which was developed in the eighteenth and nineteenth centuries, and don't imagine it is necessarily scientific, because the scientists are already beyond it. One of the first sources of this kind of thinking is Descartes. Descartes said in his search for certain knowledge that he was going to discard everything not absolutely clear to his reason and that he was going to throw out everything that he couldn't test, and that he was going to get down to the one basic idea that holds water and that cannot be disputed. The idea that he got down to was the idea, "I experience myself thinking. I know that I know." So he came up with the classic statement, "I think. Therefore I am."

This statement is certainly some kind of basis, but it resulted in a peculiar kind of consciousness which was completely different from anything that had gone before, which was strictly an individualistic consciousness. If the thinking subject is the basis of all certainty, which it is for Descartes, you get a totally different view of life from that of the Bible and what had been in Christian tradition up to that point. What happens is that the individual is a self-enclosed unit which is the starting point of everything. You start from the self-enclosed universe which thinks, and from the very beginning you have the individual enclosed within himself, seeing everything else as an object. I define myself by negating others. The other is the "not-I" and you have a universe which is "I" and "not-I." You divide everything up that way, you define yourself by separating yourself from everybody else, and then you operate and work with others from that standpoint.

Christianity came along and picked up this notion and baptized it in the sense of admitting that we are all isolated units but we should treat each other fairly and with charity. We are like billiard balls bumping against each other. The American idea, which was built up in the eighteenth century, likewise assumes that that is how people are. Everybody is an individual and he operates from this center where he is completely separated from everybody else, but he still obeys the traffic laws.

The underlying idea here is that society works if everybody just observes two things: a) he seeks his own interests while b) he observes the rules. If everybody seeks his own interests while observing the rules, the good of all will be achieved. This is the basic idea behind the economics of Adam Smith on which the American way of life is built. It is the idea that you don't ride rough-shod over everybody, you respect everybody else's rights, but basically you seek your own interests. You make your pile of money, and you try to do it honestly. And your neighbor makes his pile of money. And we all get richer and richer.

This was great in the nineteenth century, but now we have reached the point where it has become so complicated and so many other things have gotten into it that it is really not like this at all. But we still act as if it were. Actually it isn't just a question of a bunch of individuals making money. Now you have huge combinations of honest and dishonest groups. You have the Mafia and you have General Motors, all equally powerful, and they are making their pile of money in totally different ways. But they are still talking as if nothing in the basic principle had changed. We are really in a great bind because we are brought up to think of ourselves as isolated individuals and we instinctively think that is the way society is. Then as Christians we come along and baptize the idea and lift it to the supernatural plane and we say we have charity for one another.

This break-up of man into separate units is true insofar as it is a view of man under sin, but it isn't the way man is supposed to be. This is what we are struggling with now in the Church. Nineteenth-century piety took over this idea and produced nineteenth-century concepts of religious community as a group of isolated individuals, each one with his or her virtues. Nobody should have too much contact with anybody else; each one is surrounded by a little fence, and everyone communicates directly with the top but not very much with each other. The superior tells each one what to do, and everything runs well if everyone does what he is told.

But the Church has now seen that this is fatal and does not work.

The individual cannot merely say that he will do what is good for himself and observe the traffic rules and that is the end. The Christian conscience goes much deeper than that, because it is the self in Christ, the self belonging to Christ.

Our self-awareness is not the awareness that we are just individuals who have been baptized, cleansed, and purified. We don't really find out who we are until we find ourselves in Christ and in relation to other people. We are not individuals, we are persons, and a person is defined by a relationship with others. Thus the Christian conscience is not just an individual conscience with Christian traffic laws, but it is a kind of collective conscience.

Some people tend to over-correct this idea and swing away from the individual notion towards a Communist view of things—that there is just one conscience for everybody, the conscience of Christ; there is one mind for all Catholics, it is the mind of the Church, and the mind of the Church is something that is outside each individual and everybody gets lost in it. But that isn't it either. The real difficulty in defining a Christian conscience is that it is neither collective nor individual. It is personal and it is a communion of saints.

From the point of view of prayer, when I say conscience I am talking of this consciousness that is deeper than the moral conscience. When I pray I am no longer myself talking to God or myself loved by God. When I pray the Church prays in me. My prayer is the prayer of the Church.

This does not apply only to liturgy; it applies also to private prayer because I am a member of Christ. If I am going to pray validly and deeply, it will be with a consciousness of myself as being more than just myself when I pray. In other words, I am not just an individual when I pray, and I am not just an individual with grace when I pray. When I pray I am, in a certain sense, everybody. The mind that prays in me is more than my own mind, and the thoughts that come up in me are more than my own thoughts because this deep consciousness when I pray is a place of encounter between myself and God and between the common love of everybody. It is the common will and love of the Church meeting with my will and God's will in my consciousness and conscience when I pray.

This does not make prayer any easier, because when you are more than yourself, as you are in praying, you go beyond just your own ideas and you have to forget a lot of your own ideas. Much that is just you has to be left behind when you pray because that is too limited. The thing that this leads us to is that the deepest consciousness of myself is not the most private consciousness, although it is private and secret, but it is not necessarily the most remote from other people. They can't see it, know it, look at it objectively, but it is in a certain sense less private because it is where I meet other people. I meet other people not only in outward contact with them, but in the depths of my own heart. I am in a certain sense more one with other people in that which is most secret in my heart than I am when I am in external relations with them. The two go together; you can't separate them.

One of the things I should say by way of parenthesis is that my own source for these thoughts is a Russian theologian. The Russians have this idea of *sobornost*, a more intimate term of collegiality, and they have always had this idea of the Church as a real communion of souls and thought and consciousness, much more than we have until recently. Incidentally this is why I think that the Russian way of prayer is maybe one of the best for us. Russian spirituality would probably be the most helpful thing to really start contemplatives grooving in this country. This Russian theologian keeps stressing the idea of the person as being more than the individual, as being in fact that which is drawn out of us when we are in contact with others in Christ, that which is drawn out of us in communion.

All prayer is communion, not only between Christ and me but also between everybody in the Church and myself. All prayer takes us into the communion of saints. Perhaps it would be helpful to think that when I am praying I am closely united with everybody who ever prayed and everybody now praying. I am completely caught up in this communion of saints and this great reality of the prayer of Christ. I am not lost or submerged in it, but I am truly myself when I am praying in union with Christ and with the communion of saints. The real Christian conscience is down on that level.

In the old days they used to talk about "the mind of the Church," and that meant that you had read the encyclicals and knew what the Pope had said and agreed with him. Now, of course, the "mind of the Church" is that if you disagree with the Pope, you represent the mind of the Church! Neither one is right. They are both superficial. What really matters is getting down into that deeper level.

The real Christian conscience is way down in this depth where one feels at the same time a complete personal conviction—it is my conviction, it is personally mine. I am free, and it is my freedom that is saying this, and at the same time I know that I am basically united with all that the saints and the Church have ever thought. You can have this and still disagree, which is the great thing. Because when Christians disagree, as they must, over accidental things, underlying it should always be this sense of security and unity in which they are united below their disagreement. This is something we really need today in the Church. Instead, people act and react purely as individuals and from individual standpoints rather than upon this basically Christian conscience which is universal and which permits individual differences.

People who love one another very well and know each other very well can disagree and even fight like cats and dogs, but yet on a deeper level they are in agreement because of their love and their knowledge of one another. So we find in this deepest conscience and consciousness where we all are really one in a certitude which is maintained not by anybody being right but by the Holy Spirit holding everybody together in love and in Christ.

What this does is not only give you a real freedom, but it also liberates you from your own limitations, whereas before you were enclosed in your limitations. That is the big difference between the deep conscience and the individualistic conscience, and the key to it is this liberation from having to be an isolated individual and having to maintain one's isolation.

When you have to protect the isolated individual standpoint, there is a lot more work to be done because it is a one-man job of constantly maintaining one citadel against the world. This other way liberates you from all that, and all you have to defend is simply the deep conviction of what you believe to be Christian truth. This also means, of course, that you are open to other people and have an ability to respond to them because if there isn't any response then you haven't reached the deep agreement.

This agreement is not something abstract. It is based on an awareness of response, an awareness of love. You know that you are basically one with everybody else in a love which underlies any possible disagreement because you experience it. And of course the place where this is experienced above all is in the liturgy.

Let's apply this idea to a real situation: where do you get distraction in prayer? Distraction in prayer is mostly on this individual level. If the consciousness with which I am praying is an individual consciousness and I am trying to maintain an individual union with God, then everything becomes a distraction. The whole world is a distraction, and I have to thrust out everything and just maintain this one little channel of communication between God and me. That's impossible. Prayer becomes a real headache because I am trying to maintain this impossibility. The thing to do is not to exclude everything but to bring it all in. Try to realize that distractions go away if you have time for them to go away. If you haven't time for them to go away, they don't have to. For example, you can pray undistractedly if you have time to let the whole thing settle down until the distractions are gone. It may take about half an hour for distractions to seep out, and if you have an hour to spend you will have the last half-hour more or less free of distractions.

What do you do with distractions? You either simply let them pass by and ignore them, or you let them pass by and be perfectly content to have them. If you don't pay any attention to them, the distractions don't remain. They are like dreams. All you have to do is go to sleep and everything starts going through your mind, but you don't realize it, you only remember part of it.

What the Buddhists do with distractions is to note them as they go by. This is in a particular phase of Buddhist training. Buddhists try to train your consciousness completely so that you are quite aware of what everything is. This is where you start: you train yourself in interpreting this awareness.

So if you are getting distractions what you do is to say, "Oh, there goes the Union Pacific; that is my grandmother," and so on. You just note it—there it is. Gradually you become aware, "I am having a distraction about this," but it is not the ultimate, it is just something you become conscious of. When you are fully able to note distractions and see them going by, then you are in a position to make a choice. You can observe them and say, "I didn't choose to have this go by here," or "It is inevitable to have this go by here." You become aware of the fact that the distraction is not really yours. And once you are aware of that, you cannot be bothered by them because distractions only cause confusion when you are in doubt. This Buddhist approach frees you so that the important thing is not whether something is going through your mind but whether or not you are free from it.

The simplest way to freedom is time. If you don't wrestle with distractions wildly and just let them go by for a while, they get less and less, and after a while there is nothing much left. But if you are concentrating too much on God as an object among other objects, then you have trouble because it is God versus other objects. But God is not an object. God is not one thing among other things, and if you set God up in contrast to everything else you are going to have insuperable trouble. If I have to maintain the idea of God against the idea of everything else, I am going to have to fight everything in the universe because sooner or later some other idea is going to pop up. But the idea of God is not God Himself, and God is not opposed to anything; God is not opposed to any of His creatures.

That is the real problem about some of the traditional books on spirituality where it is God versus creatures from beginning to end. If you get into that, there is no hope. You will never get out of it. You have to take God and creatures all together and see God in His creation and creation in God and don't ever separate them. Then everything manifests God instead of hiding God or being in the way of God as an obstacle.

Apply that now to what I said about conscience. It is a false conscience which says, here I am and here is God and here are 10,000 objects and I must maintain free communication between God and me while all these objects are trying to stop it. You cannot pray like that.

What you have to do is have this deeper consciousness of here I am and here is God and here are all these things which all belong to God. He and I and they are all involved in one love and everything manifests His goodness. Everything that I experience really reaches Him in some way or other. Nothing is an obstacle. He is in everything. Then I don't have to fight it. And if I see it in that way, then gradually the things He really wants me to know will come from the depths of my heart. If I let things be, God will make clear what He wants me to understand and what He wants me to know. The great thing is just to leave things quiet, let them come, and let them develop as they will. If you let things alone and give yourself time and are patient and attentive and open to God, you will find that after an hour of prayer it has been good and worthwhile even if you don't know how or why.

The Church is made up of people who have all different degrees of this kind of awareness of God, some more and some less. The tone of Christian conscience in the Church is set by those who are most aware of this, and they are, strictly speaking, the saints. But religious should be, whether or not they are saints, people who are striving to keep alive this deepest kind of consciousness in the Church. This is especially so of contemplatives.

The contemplative is not somebody who can professionally turn a switch and get the prayer of quiet. The contemplative is somebody who has this Christian conscience on the deepest level so that he or she is recognized instantly by others as somebody who knows, somebody who is tuned in. Here is the Church. That is what is expected of you. People can come to you and say, "Here are people who are real Christians and have the real Christian conscience, they have the real 'mind of the Church' because they pray and prayer gives them this sense of the realities." That is your job in the Church and it is my job in the Church. It is our job that we should simply be people of whom anybody who comes to us should feel, "This is the genuine article." It isn't a particular brand of external Catholicism; it is true Christianity.

This is what Christ came on earth for—to give people this kind of freedom, this kind of simplicity, this kind of assurance of the deep realities, an assurance that there is something here.

A very simple expression of this is the man in the Gospel who said, "I was sick and a man called Jesus came along and now I am well." For us it is a little deeper than that. It is the message that I have found Christ and I am happy about it. That is what people expect of us. They come to us and find that this is real, it isn't phony. This shows, of course, why our life depends entirely and above all on prayer, because it is in prayer that this kind of deep consciousness is developed.

Nevertheless each one has to pray in such a way that it is personally real. It is not just a question of a system that everybody has to conform to. In so doing, each one of us is more than himself and more than herself. We always have to keep the lines of communication open so that we are not just us, but Christ in us and the Church in us and we are open to this whole reality of truth which is the mind of the Church in its deepest sense. It is not just what some authority said in the same words that this authority used, nor is it the mechanical repetition of what somebody has demanded of you. It is this much deeper experience of the truth of Christ, lived and experienced in our life. The apostles were the people who could come to others and say, "I know Christ, I saw Him, I walked with Him." Saint John says, "We have seen and handled the Word of life." We can't say that in those terms, but nevertheless we should be the people that someone comes to for the knowledge of Christ. In the depths of our fully developed Christian conscience there is this knowledge of Christ because we are more than just ourselves. This comes from communion, sharing together the presence of Christ.

The Life that Unifies

One of the reasons why the term "contemplative" is unsatisfactory is that in communities—groups gathered together in Christ and living the monastic life—it is not necessarily true that everybody will be a contemplative in the strict sense. There are people in monastic communities who get disturbed if you say "contemplation" and say it too loud and too hard. They may be, in a simple way, contemplatives themselves, and they think you mean something much more complicated than you really do. When you say "contemplative" they seem to think you must mean visions, that they have to be in a high state of spiritual enthusiasm. Something in them rebels against this, and it should, because that is not what we are talking about at all. Contemplation is really simple openness to God at every moment, and deep peace. And when you say

[Original editor's note: The above material is an adaptation of a taped conference given by Fr. Louis, O.C.S.O. (Thomas Merton), at a Day of Recollection. He was, primarily, a writer, one who needed little or no editing, not a speaker and this talk was quite informal. So the editor has tried to remove the repetitions that one uses for spoken emphasis; to cut away some of the words that tend to obscure the strength of the message that he was delivering—a message that undoubtedly came through very clearly because of his actual presence. The transcript of the original tape is on file at the Thomas Merton Studies Center in Bellarmine College, Louisville, Kentucky, for those who wish to consult it.—Naomi Burton.]

"experience the mysteries of Christ," it just means a deep realization in the very depths of our being that God has chosen and loved us from all eternity, that we really are His children and we really are loved by Him, that there really is a personal bond and He really is present. This is so simple that there is no need to make a commotion about it.

It is even worse if you use the term "mystic." This causes a great deal of consternation. Of all the people who should know what mysticism is and what a mystic is it should be those of us who are called to be contemplatives, and yet you have to be very careful about how you talk of mysticism in our monastic communities. It is wiser not to talk about it sometimes. Although it is perfectly right that there are mystics in contemplative communities, often it is better if they don't know it, because real mysticism is something very simple and it should remain simple. The worst thing that can happen is for a person to say, "I am a mystic; Father said in the confessional that I was really a mystic." This is not only useless; it is harmful because it means that one reflects upon one's self as an object. I want to make it quite clear that the whole essence of contemplative prayer is that the division between subject and object disappears. You do not look at God as an object and you don't look at yourself; you are just not interested in yourself. That is the real point. All this we have to keep in mind, and we have got to face it courageously.

It is unfortunate that there should be so many contemplative and monastic communities in which no one dares to discuss these matters and admit that they often do exist. Everything gets pushed over into some other aspect of the life, whereas this is the real aspect of life, the real contemplative and prayerful aspect of life.

There is a more practical approach to the real aim of our life.

You can sum it up in many different ways, and I would suggest that you do this for yourselves some time. Sit down and think: How would I define the real aim of my life—what would be the one word that I would choose? I suspect that everybody would say "love" or "union with God." One of the oldest and most traditional expressions is the word "unity." The contemplative life and the monastic life "unify," both in terms of community—a unity of persons in a community—and also unity within myself, the unification and the simplification of my whole personal being and the unification of all my heart and strivings in the one thing that is necessary, and that is the love of God.

There is another aspect of this unification: I know a psychoanalyst who is a Persian Muslim, very much interested in Persian mysticism. There are some wonderful mystics in Persia and in the Islamic world, who are called Sufis. (Their name really means that they are people who would wear wool, because they did wear wool clothes.) They were probably influenced by Christian monasticism, but they were not out of the world, but mystics living in the world in small communities, not formally organized. They did not live in one building, but came together for meetings. This pattern is found in certain parts of Asia today, and I hope I am going to visit some of these people in Indonesia. There is a man there who is known publicly as a very important lawyer in an Indonesian city. But what he really is is the leader of a mystical group that very strongly emphasizes meditation which, they say, is most necessary for their country, because it has a spiritual mission, and if there are not people praying and meditating, the country will not fulfill that mission. It would be wonderful if in this country there were such people—lay people with that sort of outlook, who would like to meditate.

My Persian friend wrote a book on psychoanalysis which begins with the idea that we should try to understand it in terms of man's highest development. Instead of orienting psychoanalysis to getting people out of trouble and getting them lined up with the rest of society, what we should really be doing is leading people to the highest perfection. Then he goes into the Sufist mysticism and its purpose—he calls it final integration—a final unification in which the person becomes fully and completely himself as he is intended to be, which is to say, a full and complete lover. Sufism is very strong on love of God, and the Sufi mystics are full of beautiful and lyrical songs of love for God and union of the soul with God. When this author speaks of final integration he says that real maturity is for a person to become a mystic. This is what man is made for. That is quite an unusual concept. You don't find too many American psychoanalysts saying that, but there is quite a large group of people in the field of psychology in this country who have become interested in this. The interest in mysticism today is found mostly in the universities where psychologists and psychoanalysts are studying mysticism with government and foundation grants, and they are much more interested in it than the theologian. The theologians are fighting over controversial ideas that really don't touch the heart of man so deeply.

Some of the psychoanalysts speak of the necessity of what they call "peak experiences," which means that it is necessary for man's total health and development that he should sometimes be not just his normal self, but beyond that—as the kids now say, "turned on." That he be really enthusiastic and happy about something just because it is, not because it does any good to him, but just because it is. And of course ultimately this means a total happiness just because God is. Sometimes we can be struck by simple truths which are usually abstract truths to us. "Jesus lives," we say to ourselves. "He is alive"—and sometimes it really lifts us up. We can't experience it all the time, but at times these truths hit us with great force and at other times they don't hit us at all, which is normal too.

This author would say that such peak experiences in the religious sphere are very good. People outside organized religion look at us and say, "They are just going to church; it is mere routine; what is the matter with their religion? Why aren't they ever turned on?" Now, actually, we are trying to be a little more lively and not just, as in the past, keeping everything under our hats. We spread a little more joy around and that is good. But here is this idea of final integration, or final unification of the person in love—really it is in a love that takes him beyond the limits of himself. The person who is not finally integrated cannot be fully himself. He must hold himself back in order to fit in with what everyone else is doing and thinking. If he does get some spiritual ideas that others don't seem to appreciate, he gives them up; he can't allow himself to feel that way or think that way—he has to keep it down to an ordinary level, and that can really hamper people. You should be able at times to allow yourself some completely personal experience of something that affects you very deeply and we should help one another to realize this. The purpose of monastic life is to create an atmosphere in which people should feel free to express their joy in reasonable ways. This final integration and unification of man in love is what we are really looking for. In other words, what should be happening in a monastic or contemplative community is that *unusual* people should be developed. This, of course, can be a problem because the person who thinks himself extraordinary is probably eccentric. What I mean is, there should be unusually good people, unusually developed people who don't know that they are or who don't care one way or the other. They are simply not

147

interested in themselves. That is the real justification of the contemplative life.

There was an old Father at Gethsemani—one of those people you get in every large community, who is regarded as sort of a funny fellow. Really he was a saint. He died a beautiful death and after he died everyone realized how much they loved him and admired him, even though he had consistently done all the wrong things throughout his life. He was absolutely obsessed with gardening, but he had an abbot for a long time who insisted he should do anything but gardening, on principle; it was self-will to do what you liked to do. Father Stephen, however, could not keep from gardening. He was forbidden to garden, but you would see him surreptitiously planting things. Finally when the old abbot died and the new abbot came in, it was tacitly understood that Father Stephen was never going to do anything except gardening, and so they put him on the list of appointments as gardener, and he just gardened from morning to night. He never came to Office, never came to anything, he just dug in his garden. He put his whole life into this and everybody sort of laughed at it. But he would do very good things—for instance, your parents might come down to see you, and you would hear a rustle in the bushes as though a moose were coming down, and Father Stephen would come rushing up with a big bouquet of flowers.

On the feast of St. Francis about three years ago, he was coming in from his garden about dinner time and he went into another little garden and lay down on the ground under a tree, near a statue of Our Lady, and someone walked by and thought, "Whatever is he doing now?" and Father Stephen looked up at him and waved and lay down and died. The next day was his funeral and the birds were singing and the sun was bright and it was as though the whole of nature was right in there with Father Stephen. He didn't have to be unusual that way: that was the way it panned out. This was a development that was frustrated, diverted into a funny little channel, but the real meaning of our life is to develop people who really love God and who radiate love, not in a sense that they feel a great deal of love, but that they simply are people full of love who keep the fire of love burning in the world. For that they have to be fully unified and fully themselves—real people.

I want to bring to your attention this book of Martin Buber's, *The Way of Man*, in which Buber takes stories from the Jewish mystics and develops them very simply. This particular story goes something like this: A disciple of a Jewish mystic wants to fast and he decides not to eat or drink anything for a week. He goes through six days and on the last day, tormented with thirst, he almost gives in and goes to the spring to take a drink. But he overcomes the temptation and turns back. As he leaves the spring he feels proud of overcoming himself, so he says, "Perhaps it would be better if I took a drink—then I would not be proud." He turns around, goes back to the spring and just when he is about to drink, he notices that he is no longer thirsty, so he says, "Why take a drink?" The next day he goes to see his Master and tells him triumphantly that he fasted for a whole week, and the Master, who has supernaturally seen all that took place, looks at him and says, "Patchwork!" In other words, you didn't do a good job at all.

Buber in commenting says, "Well, maybe that was not fair. After all, he did fast for a week; he yielded to human weakness a little bit, but he overcame himself." But the point Buber goes on to make is interesting and useful—most of our work is patchwork. It gets done finally, but it is put together in bits and pieces and that is not final integration. While we still act in this way, we are not really fully developed. We are not fully grown in the spiritual life if we have to shilly-shally back and forth. The fully integrated man should work in one piece, not patchwork, and Buber says that we can be unified beyond this stage. Too often we are content with patchwork; we get by with it—good! And if we do, all right, so much the better. Thank God for it. But there is more than that. We can do a better job; we can become totally unified; we are not helpless even though too often we get the feeling that the best we can do is muddle through.

Buber talks about the man who has a "complex self-contradictory temperament"—of which I could tell you much because that is a perfect description of me. It is rough to live with that kind of temperament, but a number of people have it and one should not feel too condemned to be complex and self-contradictory forever. He says that in the core of our soul the Divine force in its depth is capable of acting on the soul, changing it, binding the conflicting sources together, amalgamating the diverging elements. It is capable of unifying it. He makes it quite clear that there is in the depths of our souls a power of God which can do this if we let it.

If we really want to be saints in the full sense of the word, we must let God's power really work on us, and build us into one piece. But we don't do that; we evade it one way or another, and this kind of evasion is almost universally accepted. If you are getting by, fine, you are not sinning so you must be virtuous; be glad of that. No, it *is* possible and we know in our hearts that it should be possible and want it to be possible, but it is by the Divine power, not by our own power. We are afraid to believe that this power is in us. But if we do admit that this Divine force is present in our souls, it is not that we will automatically be asked to do something inhumanly difficult. It is just that we have to transcend ourselves—

we will have to go beyond our present level. Too often we are content to maintain a fairly decent level and never surpass it. But our life demands breakthroughs; not every day, not every week, not every month, but once in a while we must break through and go beyond where we are. You have to build up all you have done and push through with it, and then you find that you are out of the woods in a new clearing, you are somewhere else developing a new way.

Here is the point, and this is very important for everybody. This unification is necessary and God pushes us into it when He is going to ask us to do something unusual. Buber says that this unification must be accomplished before a man undertakes some unusual work. Only with a united soul will he be able so to do it that it becomes not patchwork but all of a piece. We get into trouble so often by finding ourselves thrown into something big that has to be patchwork because we are not ready for it; but on the other hand when the whole thing is in God's hand, He works all the elements together. You very often find that when you are entering upon something difficult you may get sick. When I entered Gethsemani, I had the worst cold I ever had in my life, and I had so much to do just to live through that cold that I could not think about anything else. By the time I got over it I was adjusted to Gethsemani. I just survived to get to choir and back, to get to work and back. Very often a sickness at a crucial point in one's life is sent by God simply to force you to get unified. You simply must concentrate on getting well and you forget everything else and then when you recover you suddenly find that everything else has dropped away. So God works on us in that way. When we are scared about something coming up that is going to be too hard, we try to get away from it. We are running away from precisely what God is using to unify us. It may be something tough that is going to demand everything in us; we may really have to put out to do it, but if we do make the effort we come through much bigger than we were before, much more developed, much more ready for something. The point Buber makes is that unity of soul can never be achieved in the middle of a job. If you plunge into something big that must be done, and you are not yet unified, it is going to be patchwork.

Buber adds that people make the mistake of thinking that unification can be achieved by asceticism, and it cannot. Simply making a resolution to do something difficult and then doing it does not protect the soul from its own contradictions. There is something much deeper than that. There is something that God has to bring about, and we can't trust in asceticism to do it. He adds another point: this unification is never final—it is always partial. There is always a little more unification to be achieved. Each time we do something with a united soul, we develop a little further. It is a sort of capital, money in the bank, so to speak, for the future. Next time we can do things better. Buber says that any work that I do with a united soul reacts upon my soul, acts in the direction of new and greater unification and leads me to a steadier unity. Thus man ultimately reaches a point where he can rely upon his soul, where he can trust, act with confidence.

That, I think, is something which we should all keep in mind. And this is what we lose when we are overburdened. There are so many little things to be done, there is such confusion, that you get lost in it, but on the other hand, the power of God is there. His power is in the depths of our soul and we are stronger than we think, not because *we* are strong, but because God is strong in us. We have to believe that. When Buber says unification of the soul, remember that the word "soul" is a special kind of word; it does not just mean the soul as the form of the body. When he talks of soul, he means the whole man—a real man. A person is real when he is a soul.

Sufism, incidentally, has some interesting things to say about who and what man is and about anthropology. Sufism divides man up in terms of his knowledge of God, his faculty for knowing God. For example, Sufism looks at man as a heart and a spirit and as a secret, and the secret is the deepest part. The secret of man is God's secret; therefore, it is in God. My secret is God's innermost knowledge of me, which He alone possesses. It is God's secret knowledge of myself in Him, which is a beautiful concept. The heart is the faculty by which man knows God and therefore Sufism develops the heart.

For us, the education of a monastic person is the education of the heart. The novitiate formation should be the formation of the heart to know God. This is a very important concept in the contemplative life, both in Sufism and in the Christian tradition. To develop a heart that knows God, not just a heart that loves God, but a heart that knows God. How does one know God in the heart? By praying in the heart. The Sufis have ways of learning to pray so that you are really praying in the heart, from the heart, not just saying words, not just thinking good thoughts or making intentions or acts of the will, but from the heart. This is a very ancient Biblical concept that is carried over from Jewish thought into monasticism. It is the spirit which loves God, in Sufism. The spirit is almost the same word as the Biblical word "spirit"—the breath of life. So man knows God with his heart, but loves God with his life. It is your living self that is an act of constant love for God and this inmost secret of man is that by which he contemplates God, it is the secret of man in God himself. This is a very, very deep concept of man, and someday I hope to study these texts further and write more about it because it is one of the deepest and best concepts that I have come across in a long time.

If I don't get around to that writing—the Sufis have this beautiful development of what this secret really is: it is the word "yes" or the act of "yes." It is the secret affirmation which God places in my heart, a "yes" to Him. And that is God's secret. He knows my "yes" even when I am not saying it. My destiny in life—my final integration—is to uncover this "yes" so that my life is totally and completely a "yes" to God, a complete assent to God. When you see the contemplative life and the monastic life in that sense, you can see how they work together. The monastic life is the setting in which by obedience, poverty, the Rule, prayer, we are set up for constantly saying "yes," but the contemplative life is the inner "yes" itself. It is the real personal response, and I think that brings the two elements perfectly together.

Here is one more quotation from one of the ascetic rabbis of the seventeenth century: "No matter how low you may have fallen in your own esteem, bear in mind that if you delve deeply into yourself you will discover holiness there. A holy spark resides there which, through repentance, you may fan into a consuming flame, which will burn away the dross of unholiness and unworthiness." That spark of holiness is the "yes" which, according to this view, cannot be extinguished. And this is also the Christian view. Deep in our hearts is the most profound meaning of our personality, which is that we say "yes" to God, and the spark is always there. All we need to do is to turn towards it and let it become a flame. This is the way we are made, and the monastic life and the contemplative life should be built on this religious conception of man which you do not find in ordinary psychology. (Though some of the psychologists are now moving towards it and adopting it, saying that this is the real point, although for them it is metaphor, poetry.) There are almost infinite potentialities in this concept and we must realize that what we are here for is to develop them. There is so much in us that can be brought out if we let God do it.

If someone is living in an unconditional "yes" to God's love, he or she is fully living what they came to religion for. Nothing else really matters once that is taken care of. Everybody can do this—people not in religious life, too—it is simply the Christian way of life.

For us, everything else should be stripped away so that we are acting more consciously and more continuously than others; that is what we really must do. We may have meaningless moments, but we can't feel totally meaningless. Down deep in you there is something that sustains you because you are letting it sustain you, and, if you let it, it will.

Prayer and the Priestly Tradition

The absolute seriousness of the love of Christ for His priests is a fact. I cannot emphasize this fact enough. This real love of Christ calls for the deepest possible response.

Today, the only way we priests can live and keep our sanity amidst all the complications of life is by breaking through to the deeper level of simplicity. The real level of course is the level of death, and that can only be reached by prayer.

"It is not ourselves we preach but Jesus Christ as Lord, and ourselves as servants for Jesus's sake. For God, who said, 'Let light shine out of darkness,' has shown in our hearts, that we in turn might make known the Glory of God shining on the face of Christ" (2 Cor. 4:5-6).

Here St. Paul is saying that not only must we announce Jesus Christ but we must know and experience this Glory of God which has been communicated to us in Christ in an ineffable way, and consequently, this is what we must communicate to the world.

Too often instead of announcing Christ we are apologizing for Christ. This is one of the sad facts about the turmoil in contemporary Christianity. All of a sudden we say such things as, "You know it's not all that serious when we present Christ. Christ is only trying to help us solve our sociological problems, and so on and

157

so on." We try to get around the seriousness of Christ, the seriousness of the Cross, and we transform them into dimensions which
suit the secular world, the press, and so forth.

This is not right: this we cannot do. We don't apologize for
Christ, we simply announce Christ as a fact. This has happened:
The Lord has come. His Kingdom has been established, this is it
and we're part of it, and we're living as Risen and Redeemed people
in Christ.

The New Creation has begun, why then apologize for it? This is
the fact, all we can do is state it, but you have to back up this statement by your own personal experience of what it means, and this
can only be gained by personal prayer and in the love of God in
Christ and of your fellow pilgrims in Christ.

Christianity is not a social philosophy nor a political mystique
like Marxism. The great power of Marxism in the world today is
that it presents itself as a complete package explanation of what
everything is all about; by adding a little dash of program, we try
to fit in our idea of Christianity.

Christianity has nothing to do with any political mystique of
any kind. This is an absolute illusion. Neither should we simply
preach a psychological formula of inner peace: Do-this-and-
you'll-forget-your-troubles attitude. Christianity does not make
you forget your troubles, it brings trouble, and we have to face
this fact.

To be a Christian today is to be in trouble. The Church is challenged, we are challenged as priests and religious, but we have to
live in this trouble on the deepest level, not on the level of apo-
logetics, but on the level of faith and personal commitment to
Christ. We must announce the Person of Christ, not certain
formulae.

As priests and Christians who, really, are we? What is our identity? What is the core within our personality? This we must find.

Remember we are called into being as fully Christian persons by a personal act and choice of Christ and of His personal love for us. The core of our personality in its fullest possible and in its most fully developed sense is our response to this Divine Love. A Divine Love directly from God and a Divine Love acting through other human beings who are brought together in the Holy Spirit and in Christ.

This is where we are. However, in order to act on this level we have to know the Person of Jesus Christ, not about Christ or about the Cross or explaining how it took place; we have to know Christ and respond personally to Him as the one in whom all the promises of the Father are fulfilled. We've got to think much more deeply about the promises of Christ.

We can be easily trapped into a kind of intellectual assent even to the fact of Christ being risen. We must not live on a double level. Sure, Christ is risen. This means our problems are quite different from the way they would look if He were not risen.

And the fact that Christ is risen means that we are now living under the New Law, not the Old Law. We must not try to solve our problems without Him. We can be fooled into thinking that we can take care of ourselves with all our modern know-how, and then just go to Him on Sundays only.

The more our technological know-how grows and the more equipment is available, the more God is pushed into the periphery these days.

But this is not the issue. God is not there just to solve problems, problems or no problems. God is the center of everything and Christ is the center of everything. Hence "that we in turn might make known the Glory of God shining in the face of Christ" (2 *Cor.* 4:6–6).

In the Oriental Church this sense of the reality of God's glory understood as a force, as a light, is much stronger than in the Western Church. The mysticism of the Oriental Church takes very seriously the concept of the glory of God as a reality of experience. It is as a light, a luminous cloud, so to speak, which is experienced spiritually.

This is now fulfilled in the New Testament which we must experience. We've got to be aware of it and live it and make it part of our being.

This, then, is another expression of God's mercy. We would not have become priests unless we knew and experienced the guiding powers of God in our lives at least in a very subtle and quiet way. This always goes hand in hand with the realization of God's utter unfailing eternal mercy. That mercy is the thing, the deepest thing that has been revealed to us by God. A mercy that cannot fail.

It is precisely here we come close to a kind of center of Christian experience, a center from which we can understand everything else. This is the center to which everything else must go just like the spokes go to the center of a wheel. If we do not keep the center in mind and if we do not live in this center, everything then becomes a rat race.

What leads you into this center is a life of prayer. At this center you will experience the love and mercy of God for yourself and find your true identity as a person to whom God has been merciful and continues to be merciful.

What leads up to this discovery is self-knowledge. I must find myself. I must solve my identity crisis, if I have one, then find myself as one loved by God, as chosen by God, and visited and overshadowed by God's mercy which I now experience as totally in terms of God's mercy.

This, of course, implies that in relation to my brother he also enjoys the same kind of identity at the center of his being. This is what the story of the Bible is all about, this is the ultimate secret that came forth from the Father and is manifested in Christ, the love and mercy of God has built its tent among us in Jesus Christ and communicates to us in Spirit.

This is what the life of prayer is for. Prayer has to break into this depth where this realization of God's mystery is also an act of obedience whereby we accept ourselves as totally given; that is, that all we have comes from the Father. This is what it means to be Christ-like because this was the life of the Son of God on earth.

I do nothing says Christ but what the Father wills. He who sees me sees the Father.

What we have to do then, especially as priests, His priests, is to live such lives that we come to experience ourselves in the same Christ-like terms. The result will be that the channel of God's grace will be absolutely free and clear.

Oftentimes we may not even notice the grace of God which flows through us to others. How many times has it happened that the things we don't plan often turn out to help other people?

❦

SECOND SESSION BY FATHER THOMAS MERTON ON THE STORY OF EMMAUS (*Lk.* 24:13–35)
This is the ordinary situation of the Christian. This is the way we are from day to day. We are pilgrims, we are disciples of Christ, and this is the normal experience of ourselves as Christians, as

people who had placed all their hope in Christ, who had believed in Him, and who recognized Him as a great prophet. Yet, something has happened and we wonder: Is there something wrong? It is true, but we still wonder.

There are so many people, for example, who are tempted against faith when it is simply ordinary confusion about everyday life. To wonder if you believe is not to doubt God, it is to doubt yourself.

And they are going along with a problem, but the problem is so big that they don't see Jesus walking with them. This is the ordinary state of life, that the problems are more important than Christ. This is the ordinary condition of man. And their problem is made up of doubts, and the core of this kind of doubt is a big question mark, who is right?

Today everybody is fighting over who is right. Every side claims to have the answer. This is one of the religious facts of our time. People go into agony. It doesn't matter who's right. God is right, hang on to the Lord at this deeper level, and let all the others yell. The fidelity of God is there and I have to be faithful to Him and to my fellow man, too.

Authority claims fidelity also as both human and divine. See authority not as an abstraction but as embodied in superiors who have feelings.

Here, now, is the solution the Lord gives. A two-fold solution, two steps:

First, we have to tell ourselves what fools we are not to believe. Second, stay with Him.

First, the experience of the heart burning within you, and then the recognition of the Risen Christ.